I0411198

OCS Report
MMS 2008-013

Deepwater Gulf of Mexico 2008: America's Offshore Energy Future

Authors

G. Ed Richardson
Lesley D. Nixon
Christy M. Bohannon
Eric G. Kazanis
Tara M. Montgomery
Mike P. Gravois

U.S. Department of the Interior
Minerals Management Service
Gulf of Mexico OCS Region

New Orleans
May 2008

TABLE OF CONTENTS

FIGURES

TABLES

ABBREVIATIONS AND ACRONYMS

2-D	two dimensional
3-D	three dimensional
AC	Alaminos Canyon
AL	Alabama
API	American Petroleum Institute
AT	Atwater Valley
ATB	articulated tug barge
BA	Brazos
BBOE	billion barrels of oil equivalent
Bcf	billion cubic feet
Bcf/d	billion cubic feet per day
BOE	barrels of oil equivalent
BOE/d	barrels of oil equivalent per day
bo/d	barrels of oil per day
BP	British Petroleum
CDWOP	Conceptual Deep Water Operations Plan
CGOM	Central Gulf of Mexico
cm	centimeters
CPA	Central Planning Area
CT	compliant tower
CZM	coastal zone management
DC	DeSoto Canyon
DOCD	Development Operations Coordination Document
DP	dynamically positioned
DTS	disconnectable turret/buoy system
DWOP	Deep Water Operations Plan
DWRR	Deep Water Royalty Relief
DWRRA	Deep Water Royalty Relief Act
EA	environmental assessment
EB	East Breaks
EC	East Cameron
EEZ	Exclusive Economic Zone
EGOM	Eastern Gulf of Mexico
EI	Eugene Island
EIS	environmental impact statement
EP	Exploration Plan
EPA	Eastern Planning Area
ESP	electric submersible pump
EW	Ewing Bank
FL	Florida

FPS	floating production system
FPSO	floating production, storage, and offloading
FPU	floating production unit
FR	*Federal Register*
FSHR	free-standing hybrid risers
ft	feet
ft³	cubic feet
GB	Garden Banks
GC	Green Canyon
GOM	Gulf of Mexico
HI	High Island
HIPPS	high integrity pressure protection system
HMPE	high modulus polyethylene
HP/HT	high pressure/high temperature
in	inches
ITB	integrated tug barge
KC	Keathley Canyon
km	kilometers
km²	square kilometers
kn	knots
LA	Louisiana
LL	Lloyd Ridge
m	meters
MAZ	multi-azimuth
Mbo/d	thousand barrels of oil per day
MC	Mississippi Canyon
Mcf	thousand cubic feet
mi	miles
mi²	square miles
MMbbl	million barrels
MMBOE	million barrels of oil equivalent
MMcf/d	million cubic feet per day
MMS	Minerals Management Service
MMscf/d	million standard cubic feet per day
MOA	Memorandum of Agreement
MODU	mobile offshore drilling unit
MP	Main Pass
mph	mile per hour
MS	Mississippi
MTLP	mini-tension-leg platform

MU	Mustang Island	SM	South Marsh
N	north	SS	Ship Shoal
NDBC	National Data Buoy Center	ST	South Timbalier
NEPA	National Environmental Policy Act	TD	total depth
		TLP	tension-leg platform
NOAA	National Oceanic and Atmospheric Administration	TVD	total vertical depth
		TX	Texas
NTL	Notice to Lessees and Operators	U.S.	United States
		U.S.C.	United States Codes
NW	northwest	USCG	United States Coast Guard
OCS	Outer Continental Shelf	USDOE	United States Department of Energy
OCSLA	Outer Continental Shelf Lands Act	USDOI	United States Department of the Interior
PDQ	production, drilling, and quarters	VK	Viosca Knoll
PEA	programmatic environmental assessment	VR	Vermilion
		VLA	vertically-loaded anchor
plets	pipeline end terminations	WATS	wide-azimuth towed streamer
PN	North Padre	WAZ	wide-azimuth
PrSDM	Pre-stack depth migration	WC	West Cameron
psi	pounds per square inch	WD	West Delta
RAZ	rich-azimuth	WGOM	Western Gulf of Mexico
RP	recommended practices	WP	Well Protector
SE	southeast	WPA	Western Planning Area
SITP	shut-in tubing pressure	WR	Walker Ridge

PREFACE

This is the eighth publication that the Minerals Management Service (MMS) has released chronicling the levels of deepwater exploration, development, and production activities in the Gulf of Mexico (GOM).

This year saw a record-setting lease offering – Sale 206. This Central Gulf sale attracted approximately $3.7 billion in high bids – the most since Federal offshore leasing began in 1954. The MMS received 1,057 bids from 85 companies on 615 blocks. About 67 percent of the blocks receiving bids were located in deep water [water depths of ≥1,312 ft or ≥400 m; this report considers activities in ≥1,000 ft or ≥305 m as deep water] with approximately 34 percent of the blocks bid upon in ultra-deep water (water depths of ≥5,249 ft or ≥1,600 m; this report considers activities in ≥5,000 ft or ≥1,524 m as ultra-deep water). The sum of the high bids for deepwater blocks was over 93 percent of the total. The ultra-deepwater blocks accounted for about 54 percent of the total high bids.

Sale 224 transpired on the same day as Sale 206, and it was the first lease offering in the Eastern Gulf since 1988. The MMS received 58 bids from 6 companies on 36 blocks, resulting in about $65 million in high bids. This is the first sale where the revenue sharing provisions of the Gulf of Mexico Energy Security Act of 2006 start immediately.

The year 2007 was also a banner year for leasing activity. Sale 205 attracted over $2.9 billion in high bids by 84 companies on 723 tracts – the third largest total in U.S. offshore leasing history. Sale 204 garnered approximately $290 million in high bids by 47 companies on 282 blocks.

Deep water has continued to be a very important part of the total GOM production, providing approximately 72 percent of the oil and 38 percent of the gas in the region. At the end of 2007, there were 130 producing projects in the deepwater GOM, up from 122 at the end of 2006. In fact, 15 deepwater fields, including Atlantis, Shenzi, and several associated with Independence Hub, began production last year. When Independence Hub reaches full capacity, it will represent over 10 percent of the total GOM gas production. Proved deepwater fields now number 125, representing a 44 percent increase from the end of 2006. For the first time in history, all 20 of the highest producing blocks in the GOM were in deep water.

A record high of 15 rigs were operating in ultra-deep water. The MMS approved 15 new technologies for use in the deepwater GOM. In fact, the first floating production, storage, and offloading (FPSO) system for use in the U.S. GOM will be installed for the development of the Cascade and Chinook Fields in Walker Ridge, with first oil expected in 2010.

The MMS is a responsible steward of U.S. offshore resources by ensuring the receipt of fair market value for the sale of leases, encouraging conservation, evaluating and approving new technology, and regulating the drilling and production of fields in ever-deepening water depths.

Lars Herbst
Regional Director
Gulf of Mexico OCS Region
Minerals Management Service

INTRODUCTION

This Deepwater Gulf of Mexico 2008 Report is the latest edition of the biennial publication produced by MMS that highlights the activities and offers trend analyses and technological advancements in this important portion of the Gulf. All statistics in this 2008 report are gleaned from data as of the end of December 2007, except production volumes and rates, which were compiled through the end of December 2006 (the most recent, complete data available at the time of this publication).

The passage of the Gulf of Mexico Energy Security Act of 2006 opened new areas for leasing in the Central Planning Area (CPA) and Eastern Planning Area (EPA). The MMS also altered the administrative boundaries for all three planning areas in the GOM. These new boundaries went into effect on July 1, 2007, concurrently with the new Outer Continental Shelf Oil and Gas Leasing Program: 2007-2012 (5-Year Program), which establishes the offshore lease sales for the Nation.

Exploratory drilling in 2007 continued to be strong in the deepwater GOM, resulting in 94 wells. Recent exploration efforts resulted in the announcement of eight new deepwater discoveries (**Table 1**). Three of these discoveries were drilled in ultra-deep water – water depths greater than 5,000 ft (1,524 m). Development activities resulted in drilling 48 new wells – a 41 percent increase over 2006. Twenty-two of these wells were drilled in water depths of 7,500 ft (2,286 m) or greater, representing 46 percent of all development wells drilled in 2007.

Significant milestones have also occurred in deepwater development activity. In 2007, 15 deepwater fields began production, many of which are associated with Independence Hub. Also, MMS approved 15 new technology applications. These technology advancements include a subsea separation and boosting system, a gravity-installed anchor with mudrope forerunners, and a disconnectable, internal turret system (for use with floating production systems). The MMS and the oil and gas industry have continued to work together to revise and improve many of the API documents that serve as recommended practices to guide operational activities.

This report is divided into five sections.

The **Background** section

- new seismic technologies,
- Lower Tertiary activities,
- ultra-deepwater drilling and discoveries, and
- hydrates.

The **Leasing and Environment** section

- 5-Year Oil and Gas Program,
- leasing activities and trends,
- future leasing activities, including anticipated lease expirations, and
- regulatory and environmental issues.

The **Drilling and Development** section

- deepwater drilling activities,
- information on operational plans,
- approval of new technologies,
- deepwater development systems,
- new deepwater developments, and
- pipelines and high-integrity pressure protection systems.

The **Reserves and Production** section

- historical deepwater reserve additions,
- large future reserve additions associated with recently-announced discoveries,
- production trends and rates,
- comparison of shallow-water and deepwater production, and
- high deepwater production rates.

The **Highlights and Conclusions** section

- highlights activities that occurred in 2007,
- drilling to production lag times, and
- difficulties in evaluating deepwater leases before their lease terms expire.

Table 1 provides a listing of the 2007 announced deepwater discoveries in the GOM.

Table 1. List of 2007 Deepwater Discoveries

Project Name	Area/Block	Water Depth (ft)	Operator
Danny[1]	GB 506	2,821	Energy Resource Technology
Droshky (Troika Deep)	GC 244	2,920	Marathon
Isabela	MC 562	6,535	BP
Julia	WR 627	7,087	ExxonMobil
Magellan	EB 424	2,767	Mariner Energy
Noonan[1]	GB 506	2,715	Energy Resource Technology
Vicksburg	DC 353	7,457	Shell
West Tonga	GC 726	4,674	Anadarko

DC = DeSoto Canyon   EB = East Breaks
GB = Garden Banks   GC = Green Canyon
MC = Mississippi Canyon   WR = Walker Ridge
[1]Separate announced discoveries in the same block.

BACKGROUND

DEFINITIONS

A variety of criteria can be used to define deep water. The threshold separating shallow water and deep water can range from 656- to 1,500-ft (200- to 457-m) in water depth. For purposes of this report, deep water is defined as water depths greater than or equal to 1,000 ft (305 m). Similarly, ultra-deep water is difficult to define precisely. For purposes of this report, ultra-deep water is defined as water depths greater than or equal to 5,000 ft (1,524 m). Leasing and royalty-relief data used in this report are expressed in meters to be consistent with regulatory requirements. All other data in this report are expressed in feet, corresponding to operational considerations.

A few other definitions are useful at this point:

- *Proved Reserves* are those quantities of hydrocarbons that can be estimated with reasonable certainty to be commercially recoverable from known reservoirs. These reserves have been drilled and evaluated and are generally in a producing or soon-to-be producing field.

- *Unproved Reserves* can be estimated with some certainty (drilled and evaluated) to be potentially recoverable, but there is as yet no commitment to develop the field.

- *Known Resources* in this report refer to discovered resources (hydrocarbons whose location and quantity are known or estimated from specific geologic evidence) that have less geologic certainty and a lower probability of production than the Unproved Reserves category.

- *Industry-Announced Discoveries* refer to oil and gas accumulations that were announced by a company or otherwise listed in industry publications. These discoveries may or may not have been evaluated by MMS, and the reliability of estimates can vary widely.

- *Field* is defined as an area consisting of a single reservoir or multiple reservoirs all grouped on, or related to, the same general geologic structural feature and/or stratigraphic trapping condition. There may be two or more reservoirs in a field that are separated vertically by intervening impervious strata or laterally by local geologic barriers, or by both.

More detailed definitions may be found in the annual *Estimated Oil and Gas Reserves, Gulf of Mexico Outer Continental Shelf, December 31, 2003* report (Crawford et al., 2006).

This report refers to deepwater developments both as fields (as defined above) and by operator-designated project names. It is important to note that the total number of fields, as defined by MMS criteria, and the total number of operator-designated projects may not be the same. A field name is assigned to a lease or a group of leases by MMS so that natural gas and oil resources, reserves, and production can be allocated on the basis of the unique geologic feature that contains the hydrocarbon accumulation(s). The field's identifying block number corresponds to the first lease qualified by MMS as capable of production or the block where the primary structure is located. Therefore, more than one operator-designated project may be included in a single MMS-designated field. **Appendix A** provides locations and additional information for these fields and projects.

Note that the term "oil" refers to both oil and condensate throughout this report and "gas" includes both associated and non-associated gas.

EXPANDING FRONTIER

When the original version of this report (Cranswick and Regg, 1997) was published in February 1997, a new era for the GOM had just begun with intense interest in the oil and gas potential of the deepwater areas. At that time there were favorable economics, recent deepwater discoveries, and significant leasing spurred on by the Deep Water Royalty Relief Act (DWRRA; 43 U.S.C. §1337). In February 1997, there were 17 producing deepwater projects, up from only 6 at the end of 1992. Since then, industry has been rapidly advancing into deep water, and many of the anticipated fields have begun production. At the end of 2007, there were 130 producing projects in the deepwater GOM, up from 122 at the end of 2006 (Peterson et al., 2007).

Historically, deepwater production began in 1979 with Shell's Cognac Field, but it took another 5 years before the next deepwater field (ExxonMobil's Lena Field) came online. Both developments relied on extending the limits of platform technology used to develop the GOM shallow-water areas. Deepwater exploration and production grew with tremendous advances in technology since those early days. This report focuses on changes during the last 16 years, 1992-2007.

Over these last 16 years, leasing, drilling, and production moved steadily into deeper waters. There are approximately 7,443 active leases in the GOM Outer Continental Shelf (OCS), 54 percent of which are in deep water. (Note that lease statuses may change daily, so the current number of active leases is an approximation.) Contrast this to approximately 5,600 active GOM leases in 1992, only 27 percent of which were in deep water. There was a maximum of 30 rigs drilling in deep water in 2007, compared with only 3 rigs in 1992. Likewise, deepwater oil production rose about 820 percent and deepwater gas production increased about 1,155 percent from 1992 to 2006.

SEISMIC ACTIVITY

A combination of factors, including the DWRRA, key deepwater discoveries, the recognition of high deepwater production rates, and the evolution of deepwater development technologies, spurred a variety of deepwater activities. One of the first impacts was a dramatic increase in the acquisition of 3-dimensional (3-D) seismic data (**Figure 1**). (Note that **Figures 1 and 2** illustrate areas permitted for seismic acquisition. The actual coverage available may be slightly different than that permitted.) Three-dimensional seismic data are huge volumes of digital energy recordings resulting from the transmission and reflection of sound waves through the earth. These large "data cubes" can be interpreted to reveal likely oil and gas accumulations. The dense volume of recent, high-quality data may reduce the inherent risks of traditional hydrocarbon exploration and allow imaging of previously hidden prospects. **Figure 2** illustrates the surge of seismic activity in the deepwater GOM during the last 16 years. Seismic acquisition has stepped into progressively deeper waters since 1992. **Figure 2** shows the abundance of 3-D data now available. These data blanket most of the deepwater GOM, even beyond the Sigsbee Escarpment (a geologic and bathymetric feature in ultra-deep water). Note that many active deepwater leases were purchased before these 3-D surveys were completed [only the more sparsely populated two-dimensional (2-D) datasets were available].

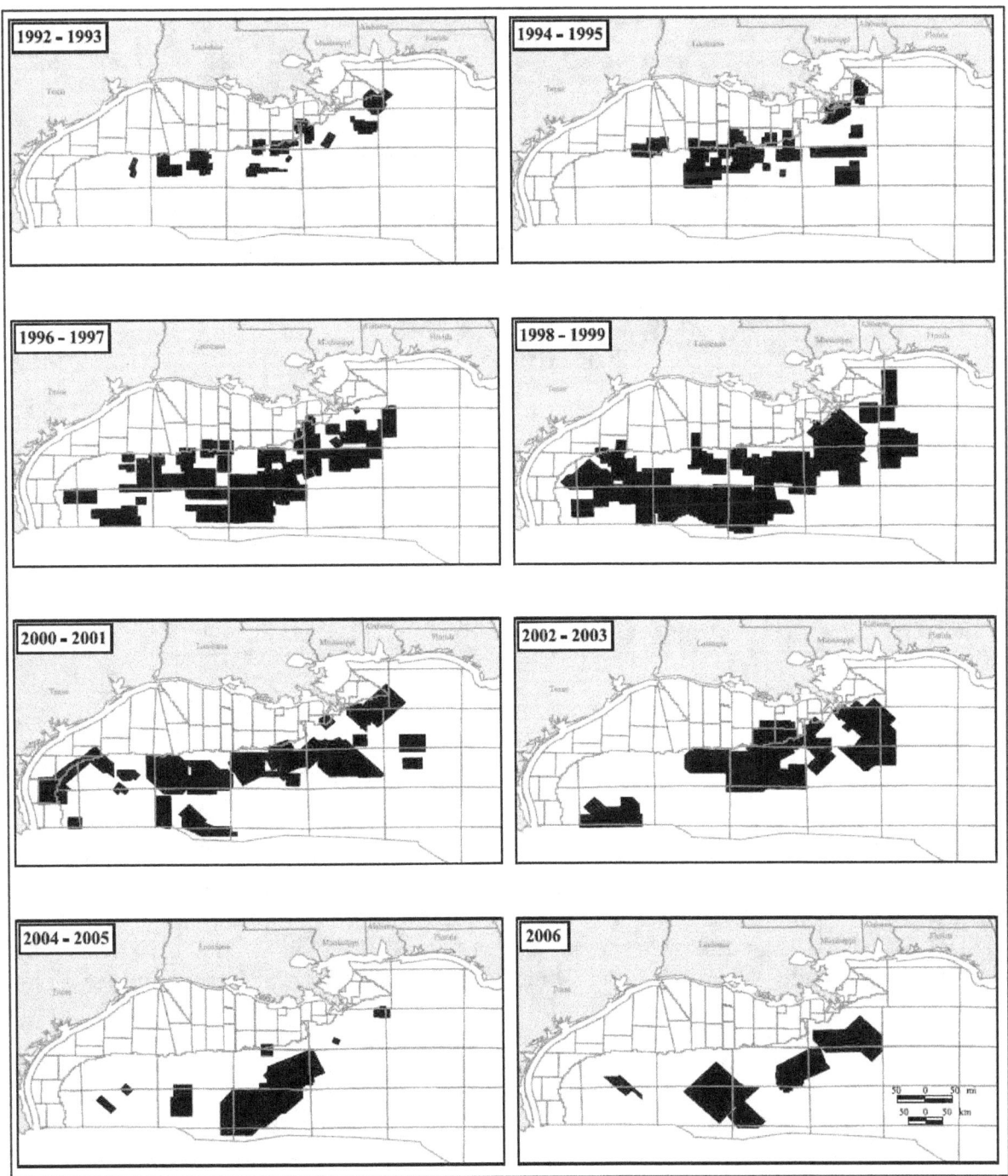

Figure 1. Progressive deepwater 3-D seismic permit coverage.

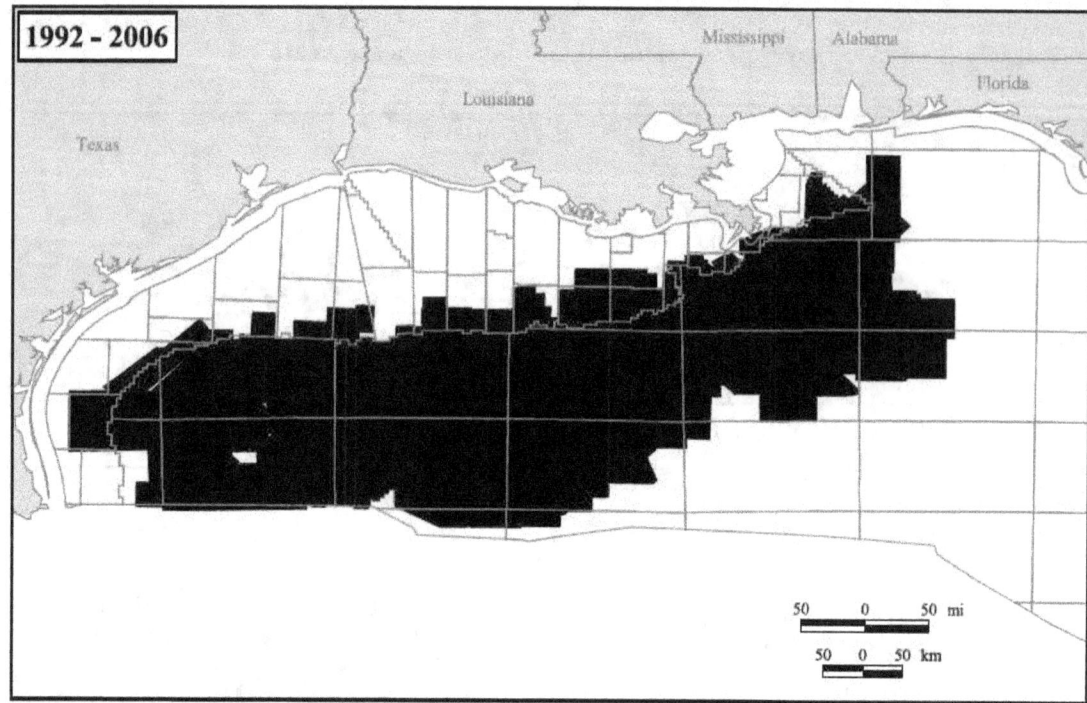

Figure 2. Deepwater 3-D seismic permit coverage from 1992 to 2006.

The seismic permitting coverage shown in **Figure 2** does not tell the whole story of geophysical activity in the deepwater GOM. Numerous deepwater exploration targets lie beneath an extensive salt canopy, more than 15,000 ft (4,572 m) thick in some places. Salt has a very high velocity when compared with the surrounding rocks, and a correction for this high velocity zone must be made to best image the sediments below the salt. Additionally, the imaging problems are compounded the thicker and more irregular the salt bodies are. As industry explored farther and farther out into deep water, one of the major technological hurdles has been obtaining quality, subsalt seismic images for adequate interpretation.

Pre-stack depth migration (PrSDM) of seismic data has greatly enhanced the interpretation capabilities in the deepwater GOM, particularly for the areas hidden below salt canopies. While PrSDM was once used sparingly, the availability of large speculative PrSDM surveys allows the widespread use of this technology in the early phases of exploration. Subsalt discoveries like Mad Dog, Thunder Horse, North Thunder Horse, Atlantis, Tahiti, and Shenzi demonstrate the importance of subsalt exploration in the deepwater GOM. **Figure 3** provides a good indication of the widespread coverage of PrSDM processing through the end of 2006. However, even with the advantages of PrSDM data, interpretation challenges, such as poor signal-to-noise ratio of the subsalt events and incomplete reservoir illumination, remained. These problems have been addressed mainly by such things as improved depth-migration algorithms, better noise attenuation, and better velocity models. However, it became apparent that another approach was needed to produce seismic images of reservoir-development quality.

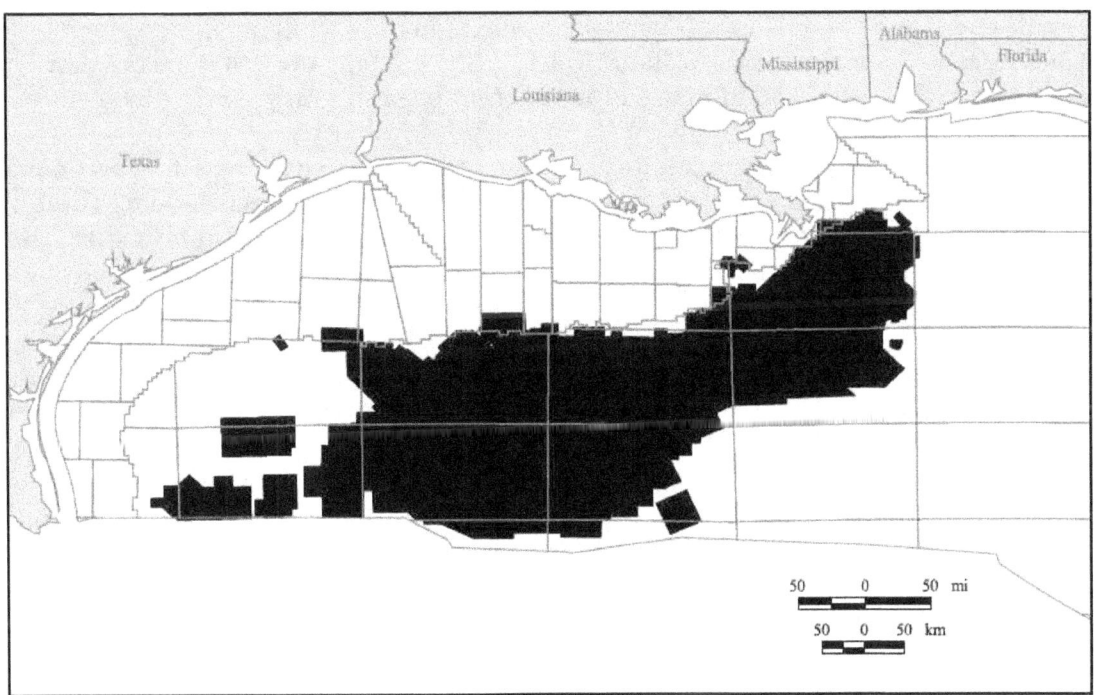

Figure 3. Pre-stack depth migration coverage from various industry sources.

Technological Advances

It has long been recognized that acquiring seismic data with a range of source-receiver azimuths illuminates the subsurface better than acquiring the same data using standard narrow-azimuth techniques (e.g., O'Connell et al., 1993). However, the technology required to make complex-azimuth acquisitions commercially viable only emerged in recent years. Three variations of towed-streamer geometries for acquiring complex-azimuth data are (1) multi-azimuth (MAZ), (2) wide-azimuth (WAZ), and (3) rich-azimuth (RAZ).

In a MAZ survey, a single multi-streamer recording vessel acquires data in multiple directions (Hegna and Gaus, 2003). Two to six 3-D surveys are recorded over the same area at different azimuths to each other. The individual surveys are processed separately, and then combined, resulting in the same subsurface spot being illuminated by many different azimuths. In a WAZ (a.k.a. WATS, for wide-azimuth towed streamer) survey, a single multi-streamer recording vessel and at least two source vessels shoot each source line multiple times in a single direction with increasing lateral offset with each sailing pass. Multiple source vessels make it possible to collect data from many different azimuths (Sukup, 2002). The RAZ geometry combines aspects of both the MAZ and WAZ methods, where multiple source lines are acquired in multiple directions. By combining the MAZ and WAZ techniques, any number of vessels in various configurations (WAZ) can be sailed in any number of directions (MAZ) (Howard, 2004).

British Petroleum, with seismic contractor Veritas, conducted the first WAZ survey in the GOM at the end of 2004 and beginning of 2005 at Mad Dog (Green Canyon 826 Field). At the beginning of 2006, Shell, with seismic contractor WesternGeco, acquired a WAZ survey over the Friesian prospect, a 2006 discovery in Green Canyon Block 599. Also contracting with WesternGeco, BHP Billiton acquired a RAZ survey during the spring and summer of 2006 at Shenzi (Green Canyon 654 Field). Additionally, WesternGeco began the first multi-client WAZ acquisition (E-Octopus project) in July 2006 in Garden Banks, Green Canyon, Keathley Canyon, and Walker Ridge. Since then, over 700 blocks have been acquired in two phases. A third phase of acquisition began in May 2007, which covers 450 blocks in Green Canyon.

With minimal processing, no multiple attenuation, and shot-domain wave equation migration using existing velocity models, initial results from the proprietary Friesian and Shenzi surveys and from the multi-client E-Octopus Phases I and II surveys show that all four survey designs lead to improved subsalt imaging when compared with conventional narrow-azimuth surveys with full processing including multiple attenuation (Kapoor et al., 2007). In general, complex-azimuth surveys improve signal-to-noise ratio and illumination in complex subsalt geology and provide natural attenuation of some multiples. Therefore, areas of the deepwater GOM where an extensive and thick salt canopy covers potential hydrocarbon targets, obscuring their seismic signature, are ideal areas for large-scale, complex-azimuth surveys for exploration purposes. In fact, other vendors, including CGGVeritas, Petroleum Geo-Services, and TGS, have acquired or are currently acquiring several multi-client WAZ surveys in the deepwater GOM.

LOWER TERTIARY ACTIVITY

Figure 4 indicates that about 99 percent of total GOM proved reserves are in Miocene and younger reservoirs; however, recent exploration activities in deep water have discovered large reservoirs in sands of Lower Tertiary age (Oligocene, Eocene, and Paleocene). **Figure 5** shows these discoveries within the bounds of the approximate Lower Tertiary trend. The trend has an estimated discovery volume of 2.8 billion barrels of producible hydrocarbons, which represents about a 15 percent addition to total GOM oil and gas volumes. It is noteworthy that this discovery volume has more than doubled since the 2007 Deepwater Report (Peterson et al., 2007).

However, unique technical challenges have required tremendous industry investment to ensure that this frontier play becomes an economically viable trend. Challenges have included complex subsalt imaging issues, drilling rig limitations, high pressure/high temperature (HP/HT) conditions, and reservoir porosity and permeability anisotropy. However, technological advances including WATS data, improved HP/HT environment equipment, and next generation semisubmersible drilling vessels, combined with promising results from the Jack #2 well test, have facilitated exploration and indicate that Lower Tertiary reservoirs have the potential to support commercial production.

Time (mya)	System	Subsystem	Series	Total Proved Reserves	Discovered BOE All Water Depths	Discovered BOE Water Depths >1,000 ft	General Deepwater Characteristics
1.77	Quaternary		Pleistocene	98.9% (52.3 BBOE)	94.2% (58.5 BBOE)	84.9% (15.6 BBOE)	Large subsalt discoveries in deepwater are associated with fold belts and turtle structures.
23.80	Tertiary	Upper	Pliocene				
			Miocene				
		Lower	Oligocene	0.4% (0.2 BBOE)	4.5% (2.8 BBOE)	15.1% (2.8 BBOE)	Over a dozen announced Lower Tertiary (Eocene/Paleocene) discoveries this decade in deepwater opened a large play area for exploration.
65.00			Eocene				
			Paleocene				
144.20	Cretaceous	Upper		0.7% (0.4 BBOE)	1.3% (0.8 BBOE)	—	There is untested, Mesozoic potential on the abyssal plain and in eastern Mississippi Canyon.
		Lower					
164.40	Jurassic	Upper					
		Middle					

Figure 4. Deepwater stratigraphic section.

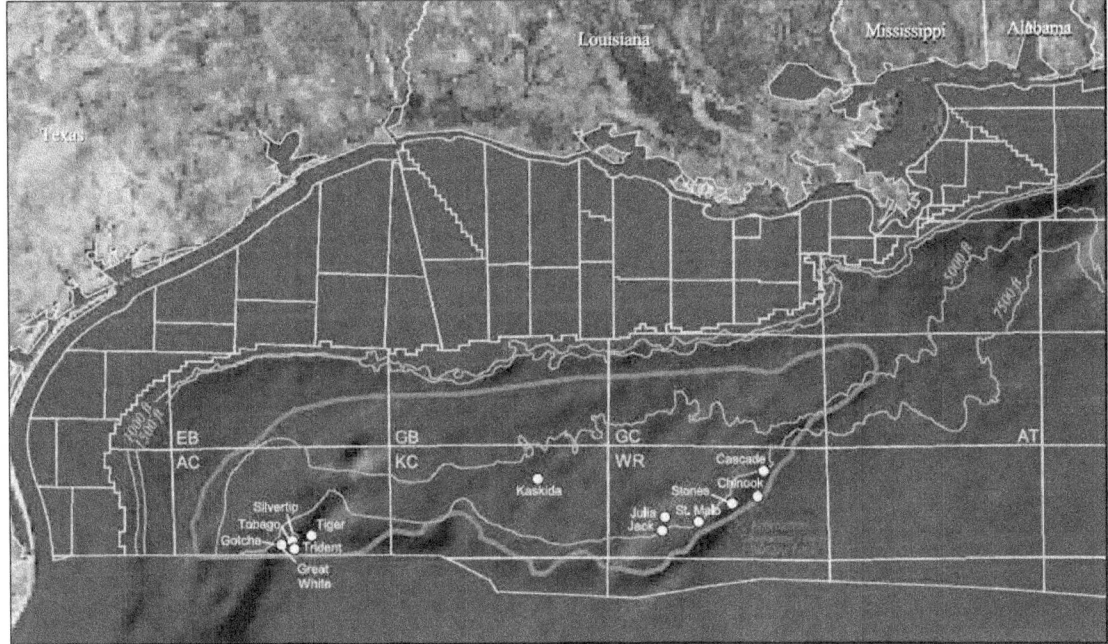

Figure 5. Deepwater Lower Tertiary trend.

Issues of water depth and proximity to current development infrastructure are being overcome through the planned use of the Gulf's first FPSO system at the Chinook-Cascade development in Walker Ridge. Additionally, an expanded pipeline network will tie into the Perdido Regional Development hub, which will produce the Great White, Tobago, and Silvertip Fields in Alaminos Canyon. Production from both projects is currently planned to begin around the end of the decade.

While attempts to forecast future Lower Tertiary production are complicated by many variables, it is clear that technical advances and exploratory successes will continue to drive industry interest in the emerging Lower Tertiary trend.

ULTRA-DEEPWATER DRILLING AND DISCOVERIES (≥5,000 FT OR ≥1,524 M)

In 2007, a record number of 15 rigs were drilling for oil and gas in water depths of 5,000 ft (1,524 m) or more in the GOM. At least 13 new drilling rigs are being built and contracted for use in the ultra-deepwater Gulf and will be ready for operation in the next 2-3 years—they will be capable of operating in water depths up to 12,000 ft (3,658 m) and drilling to total depths up to 40,000 ft (12,192 m). Also, all 13 of these new drilling rigs are being built with dynamic positioning systems and will not have to be moored to the seafloor. Additionally, several drilling contractors have committed to building new ultra-deepwater drilling rigs that have not yet been contracted, and some of these new rigs are expected to operate in the GOM.

In 1986, the first discovery in the GOM in water depths greater than 5,000 ft (1,524 m) occurred with Mensa. Since that time, there have been 60 additional discoveries in the ultra-deep provinces of the Gulf (**Table 2**). The production from 13 of these discoveries is associated with the Independence Hub natural gas processing facility. Another 14 of the discoveries are associated with the Lower Tertiary trend.

Table 2. List of Deepwater Discoveries in Water Depths Greater than 5,000 ft (1,524 m)

Discovery	Area/Block	Water Depth (ft)[3]	Discovery Year
Constitution	GC 680	5,001	2001
GC 767	GC 767	5,116	2004
Rigel	MC 252	5,227	1999
Ticonderoga	GC 768	5,259	2004
Big Foot	WR 29	5,268	2005
King	MC 84	5,303	1993
Mensa	MC 731	5,313	1986
Red Hawk	GB 877	5,329	2001
Goldfinger	MC 771	5,413	2004
Horn Mountain	MC 127	5,422	1999
Devil's Tower	MC 773	5,532	1999
N. Thunder Horse	MC 776	5,662	2000
Thunder Bird	MC 819	5,672	2006
Thunder Hawk	MC 734	5,714	2004
Kaskida[2]	KC 292	5,721	2006
Kepler	MC 383	5,741	1987
La Femme	MC 427	5,782	2004
Seventeen Hands	MC 299	5,881	2001
Thunder Horse	MC 778	6,082	1999
Thunder Ridge	MC 737	6,108	2006
Ariel	MC 429	6,134	1995
Neptune (AT)	AT 575	6,203	1995
Isabela	MC 562	6,535	2007
King's Peak	DC 133	6,541	1993
Anstey	MC 607	6,601	1997
Atlantis	GC 743	6,612	1998
Bass Lite	AT 426	6,623	2001
Herschel	MC 520	6,739	1989
Fourier	MC 522	6,895	1989
Blind Faith	MC 696	6,952	2001
Jack[2]	WR 759	6,962	2004
St. Malo[2]	WR 678	6,996	2003
Aconcagua	MC 305	7,051	1999
Mission Deep	GC 955	7,068	2006
Julia[2]	WR 627	7,087	2007
Camden Hills	MC 348	7,206	1999
Vicksburg	DC 353	7,457	2007
Shiloh	DC 269	7,509	2003
Coulomb	MC 657	7,558	1987

Table 2. List of Deepwater Discoveries in Water Depths Greater than 5,000 ft (1,524 m)

Discovery	Area/Block	Water Depth (ft)[3]	Discovery Year
BAHA[2]	AC 600	7,620	1996
Gotcha[2]	AC 856	7,714	2006
Callisto	MC 876	7,790	2001
San Jacinto[1]	DC 618	7,805	2004
Great White[2]	AC 857	8,119	2002
Q[1]	MC 961	7,926	2005
Merganser[1]	AT 37	7,939	2001
Spiderman/Amazon[1]	DC 620	8,055	2004
Spiderman/Amazon[1]	DC 621	8,087	2003
Cascade[2]	WR 206	8,152	2002
Vortex[1]	AT 261	8,344	2002
Mondo NW Extension[1]	LL 1	8,351	2005
Mondo Northwest[1]	LL 2	8,362	2004
Jubilee Extension[1]	LL 309	8,774	2005
Jubilee[1]	AT 349	8,778	2003
Atlas NW[1]	LL 5	8,807	2004
Chinook[2]	WR 469	8,831	2003
Atlas[1]	LL 50	8,944	2003
Cheyenne[1]	LL 399	8,983	2004
Tiger[2]	AC 818	9,004	2004
Silvertip[2]	AC 815	9,226	2004
Tobago[2]	AC 859	9,627	2004
Stones[2]	WR 508	9,571	2005
Trident[2]	AC 903	9,721	2001

AC = Alaminos Canyon   AT = Atwater Valley   DC = DeSoto Canyon
GB = Garden Banks   GC = Green Canyon   KC = Keathley Canyon
LL = Lloyd Ridge   MC = Mississippi Canyon   WR = Walker Ridge

[1]Projects associated with the Independence Hub natural gas processing facility.

[2]Projects associated with the Lower Tertiary trend.

[3]Average water depth of all wells drilled.

HYDRATES

In addition to the traditional oil and gas plays in the deepwater GOM, there may be significant resources in gas hydrate-bearing sands. The in-place hydrate resource may be 30 to 300 times greater than conventional oil and gas reserves. A gas hydrate is a cage-like lattice of ice that traps molecules of natural gas, primarily methane. Hydrates are formed at and just below the seafloor under conditions of low temperature, high pressure, and in the presence of natural gas. In the GOM, hydrates occur in water depths greater than 1,450 ft (442 m). Each cubic foot of hydrate yields 165 ft^3 (4.7 m^3) of gas at standard temperature and pressure.

Piston cores have sampled about 100 sites that contain both thermogenic and biogenic gas hydrates. Thermogenic gas hydrates are known only in the GOM, whereas biogenic gas hydrates are found in many other marine settings around the world. The gas contained in thermogenic gas hydrates is derived from deeply buried, organic-rich sediments, or existing gas reservoirs, and has migrated upward into the zone of hydrate stability. Thermogenic hydrates contain a mixture of complex hydrocarbon gases. Biogenic gas hydrates contain gas generated at shallower depths by bacterial decomposition of organic matter, yielding primarily methane gas. Gas-hydrate mounds and associated chemosynthetic communities, commonly at the edges of deepwater mini-basins, have been observed and sampled by research submersibles funded by the MMS at 32 sites in the GOM.

Many questions remain about the distribution, concentration, reservoir properties, and stability of hydrates. Conventional drilling operations do not allow sampling of the upper 3,000 ft (914 m) of sediment (where hydrates occur). Although conventional 3-D exploration and high-resolution seismic data are not specifically designed to detect hydrate deposits, interpretive techniques have been used to delineate possible hydrates.

To gather hydrate data for the GOM, a Joint Industry Project of MMS and seven oil and service companies, largely funded by the U.S. Department of Energy (USDOE), conducted a 35-day expedition in the spring of 2005 to drill, log, and core sediments containing gas hydrates. Five separate boreholes were drilled near seafloor hydrate mounds in Atwater Valley and Keathley Canyon to depths as great as 1,509 ft (460 m) below mudline. Two holes were cored on top of a hydrate mound in Atwater Valley to a depth of 98 ft (30 m) below mudline. Downhole log data and pressure cores revealed evidence of gas hydrates in all boreholes at levels approximating those predicted by pre-cruise seismic analysis. Sediment at both locations was fine grained with stratigraphically controlled hydrate-bearing intervals in Atwater Valley and steeply dipping, hydrate-filled fractures in Keathley Canyon. Because technically recoverable quantities of gas hydrate are probably limited to permeable sand reservoirs, a second hydrate drilling initiative with a multi-well program at sites in Green Canyon, Walker Ridge, and Alaminos Canyon is planned for 2008.

The MMS has played a major role on the site-selection team by using information from the in-house sand studies done for the Gas Hydrate Assessment. This MMS assessment is the first comprehensive evaluation of gas hydrates on the OCS since a 1995 assessment published by the U.S. Geological Survey (USGS) (Collett, 1995). Ultimately, the final results of the MMS assessment will provide estimates of the undiscovered in-place, technically recoverable, and economically recoverable gas hydrate resources for each OCS region (GOM, Atlantic, Pacific, and Alaska). As of February 2008, the preliminary in-place results for the GOM have been prepared (USDOI, MMS, 2008). Both MMS and USGS studies can be accessed at http://www.mms.gov/revaldiv/GasHydrateAssessment.htm.

LEASING ACTIVITY

The DWRRA encouraged extensive leasing in the deepwater GOM. **Figure 6** shows the history of deepwater leasing since 1992. Activity slowly increased from 1992 through 1995, but immediately after the DWRRA was enacted, deepwater leasing activity exploded. Other factors also contributed to this activity, including improved 3-D seismic data coverage, key deepwater discoveries, the recognition of high deepwater production rates, and the evolution of deepwater development technologies.

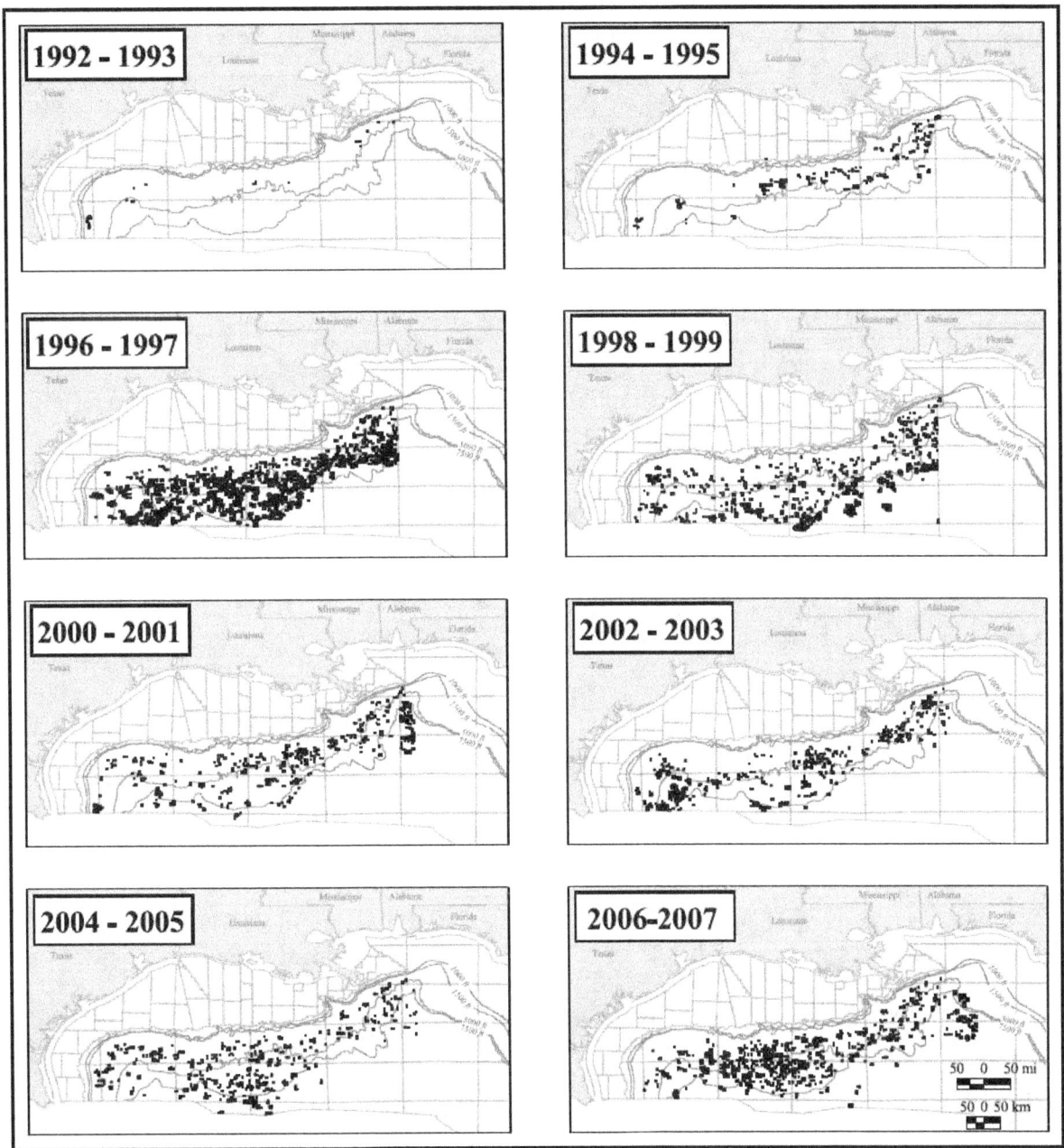

Figure 6. Deepwater leases issued.

With the passage of the Energy Policy Act of 2005, lease terms for deepwater royalty relief were changed. The Act eliminated the existing 1,600-m (5,249-ft) or deeper water-depth category for royalty relief and established two new royalty suspension categories: 1,600- to 2,000-m (5,249- to 6,562-ft) and greater than 2,000-m (6,562-ft) water depth. Sale 196 [Western Planning Area (WPA), August 17, 2005] was the first lease offering to implement these "new" royalty-relief provisions.

CHALLENGES AND REWARDS

Significant challenges exist in deep water in addition to environmental considerations. Deepwater operations are very expensive and often require significant amounts of time between the initial exploration and first production. Despite these challenges, deepwater operators often reap great rewards. **Figure 7** shows the history of discoveries in the deepwater GOM. There was a shift toward deeper water over time, and the number of deepwater discoveries continues at a steady pace.

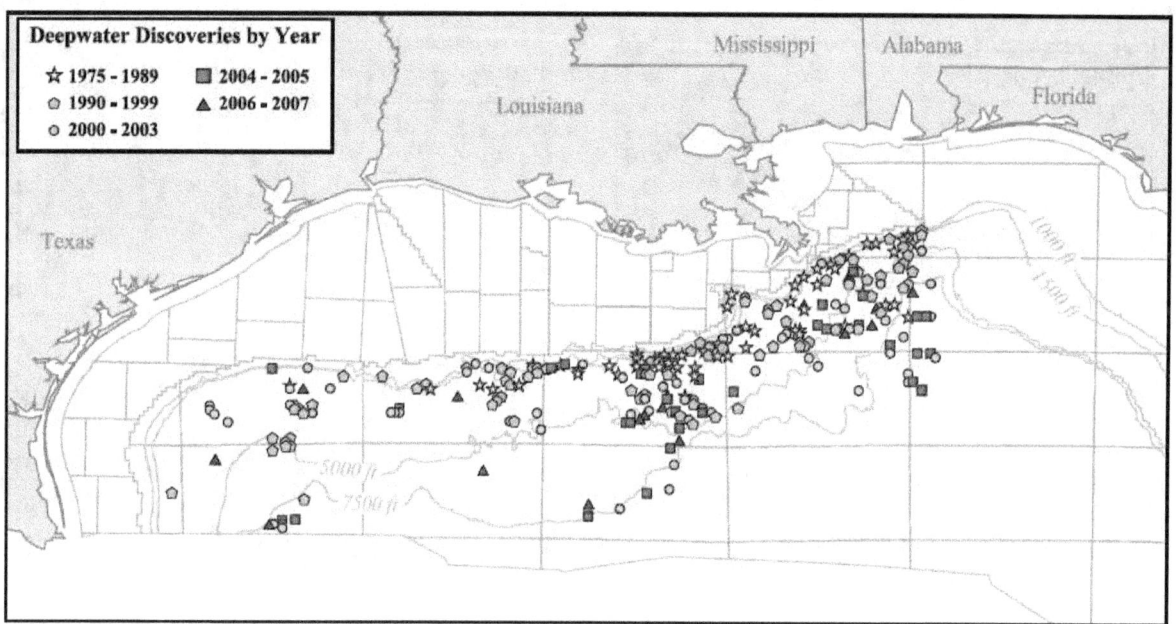

Figure 7. Deepwater discoveries.

Figure 8 shows how major and nonmajor oil and gas companies compare in terms of deepwater discoveries. In this report, we define major companies to include BP, ChevronTexaco, ExxonMobil, and Shell. The grouping of these four entities does not indicate a regulatory conclusion or an analysis of production size. It is merely a convenient category for the purpose of comparison. In the past, major companies were responsible for the majority of discoveries and led the way into the deepest waters. However, the number of discoveries by nonmajor companies has surpassed that by major companies. In addition, nonmajor companies have made numerous recent discoveries in the deepest waters of the frontier. Indeed, nonmajors announced five of the eight deepwater discoveries in 2007.

In addition to the significant number of deepwater discoveries, the flow rates of deepwater wells and the field sizes of deepwater discoveries are often quite large. These factors are critical to the economic success of deepwater development. **Figure 9** illustrates the estimated sizes and locations of 125 proved deepwater fields. This represents a 44 percent increase in the number of fields from the 2006 Deepwater Report (French et al., 2006). In addition to their large sizes, deepwater fields have a wide geographic distribution and range in geologic age from Pleistocene through Paleocene.

Figure 10 illustrates existing and potential hubs for deepwater production. For purposes of this report, deepwater hubs are defined as surface structures that host production from one or more subsea projects. These hubs represent the first location where subsea production surfaces and are the connection point to the existing pipeline infrastructure. Note that potential hubs are moving into deeper waters, expanding the infrastructure, and facilitating additional development in the ultra-deepwater frontier.

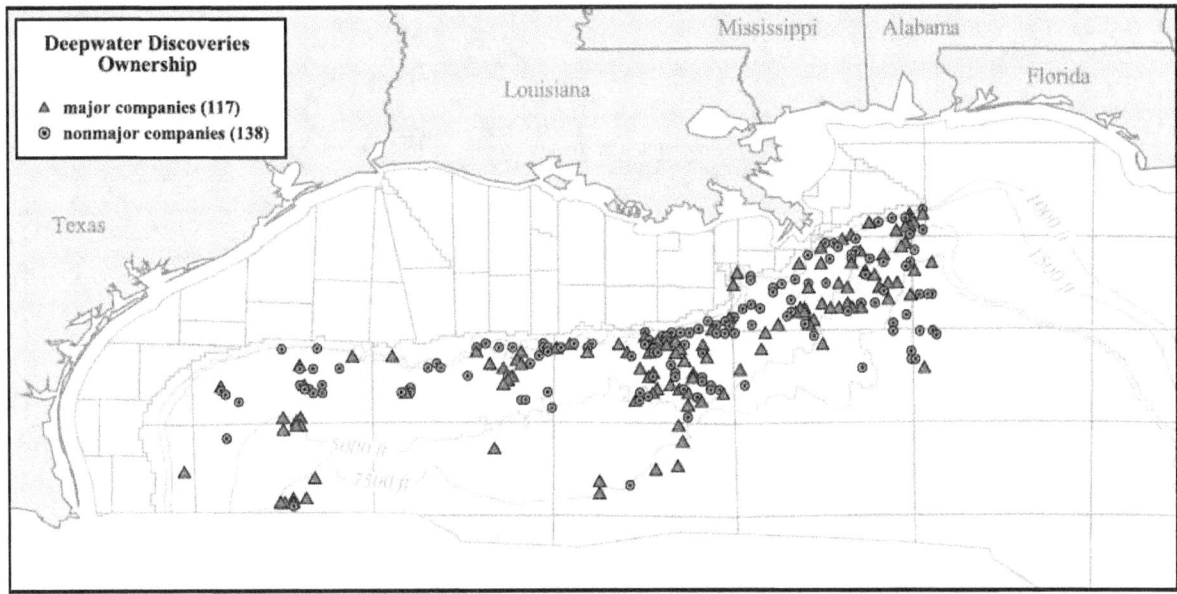

Figure 8. Ownership of deepwater discoveries (includes industry-announced discoveries).

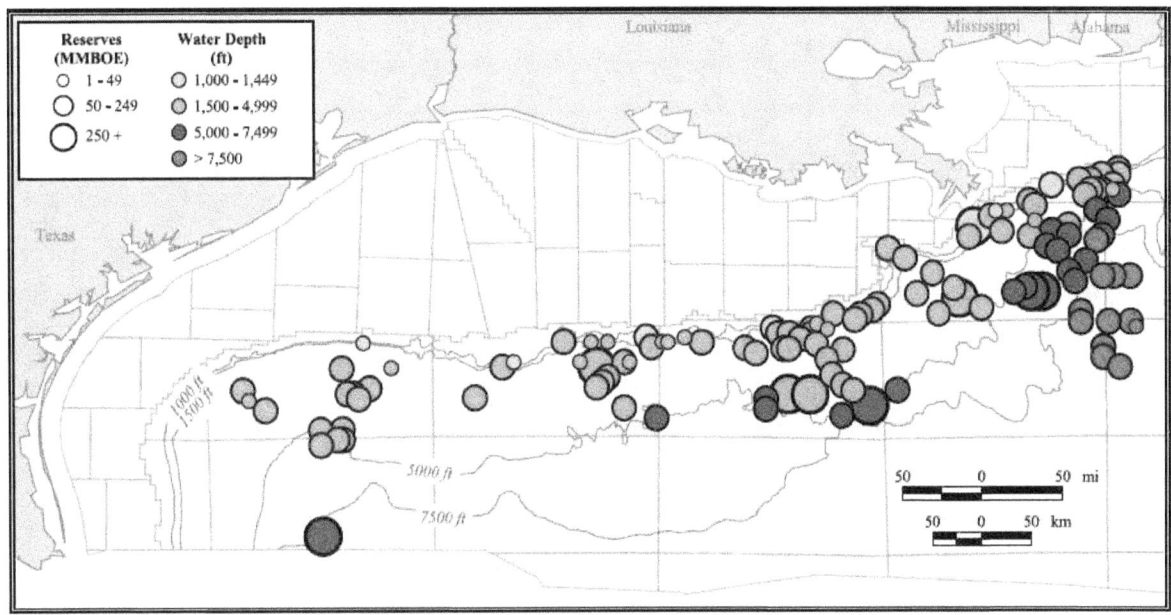

Figure 9. Estimated volume of 125 proved deepwater fields.

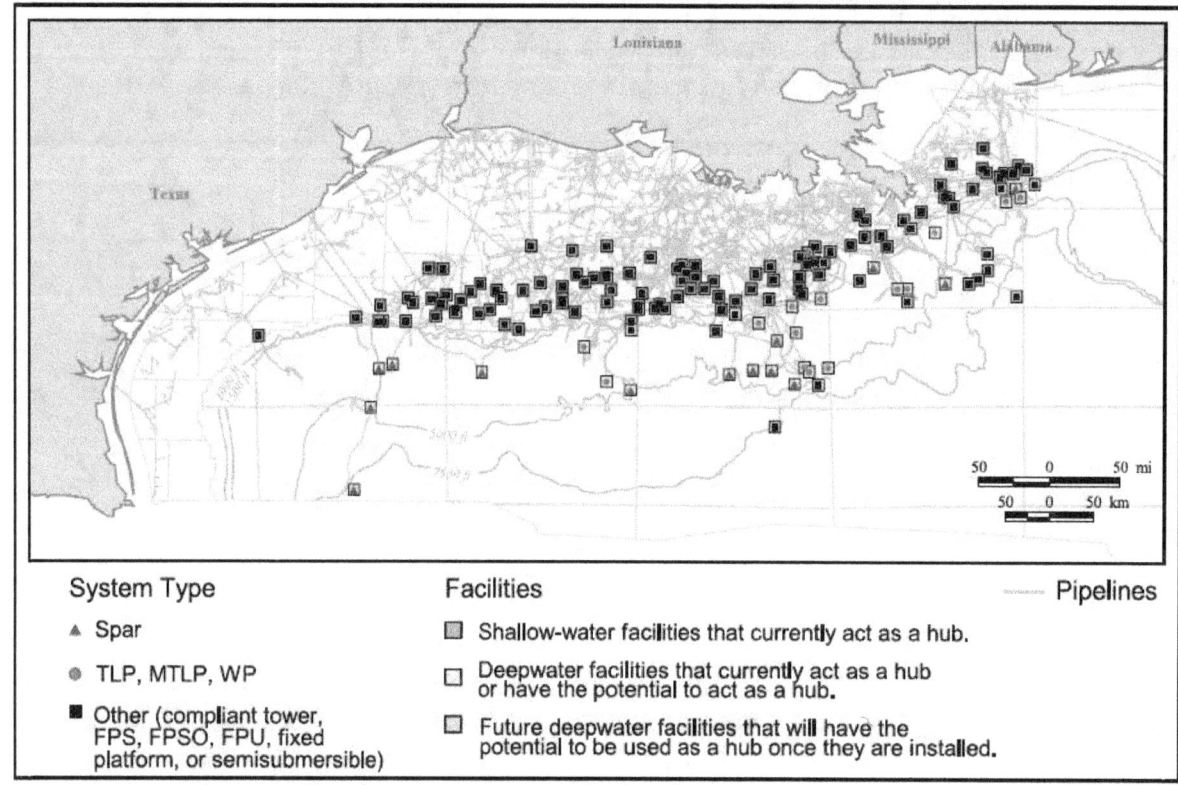

Figure 10. Current, potential, and future hub facilities.

LEASING AND ENVIRONMENT

5-YEAR OCS OIL AND GAS LEASING PROGRAM

Section 18 of the OCS Lands Act (OCSLA) requires the Secretary of the Interior to prepare and maintain a 5-year program. The program reflects a proper balance among the potential for the discovery of oil and natural gas, the potential for environmental damage, and the potential for adverse effects on the coastal zone. The 5-Year Program also must provide for the receipt of fair market value by the Federal Government for land leased and rights conveyed.

When approved, the leasing program consists of scheduled lease sales for a 5-year period, along with policies pertaining to the size and location of sales and the receipt of fair market value. The purpose of a schedule is to increase the predictability of sales in order to facilitate planning by industry, affected States, and the general public. The schedule indicates the timing and location of sales and shows the presale steps in the process that lead to a competitive sealed bid auction for a specific OCS area. To facilitate the scheduling of and preparation for sales in the 5-Year Program, the OCS is divided into administrative geographical units called planning areas.

In preparing a new 5-year program, the Secretary solicits comments from coastal State Governors and localities, tribal governments, the public, the oil and natural gas industry, environmental groups, affected Federal agencies, and Congress. The MMS requests comments at the start of the process of developing a new program and following the issuance of each of the first two versions: (1) the draft proposed program with a 60-day comment period; and (2) the proposed program with a 90-day comment period. The third and last version, the proposed final program, is prepared with a 60-day notification period following submission to the President and Congress. After 60 days, if Congress does not object, the Secretary may approve the program.

In addition to the steps required by Section 18 of the OCSLA, the Secretary must comply with the requirements of the National Environmental Policy Act (NEPA). Additional scoping may occur and an environmental impact statement (EIS) on the 5-Year Program is prepared. During the comment period on the draft EIS, public hearings are held in various coastal locations around the Nation. After the receipt of comments, a final EIS is prepared. A record of decision is prepared that formalizes the alternatives that were selected from the final EIS.

Each lease sale proposed in the program's schedule must also undergo a NEPA evaluation and presale coordination steps required by Section 19 of the OCSLA. An environmental assessment that is specific to the individual lease sale is usually prepared. These documents examine new information and changes that have occurred since the final EIS was prepared. Consultation is conducted with the States during the process and consistency with each affected State's Coastal Zone Management (CZM) program is determined before the lease offering transpires.

The listing below shows the major sequential steps in the process after adoption of a 5-year program.

- Call for Information and Nominations; Notice of Intent to Prepare an EIS

- Area Identification

- Draft EIS

- Public Hearings

- Final EIS and CZM Consistency Determination

- Record of Decision

- Sale-specific NEPA evaluation

- Proposed Notice of Sale

- Governor's Comments

- Final Notice of Sale

- Sale

- Decision to Accept or Reject Bids

- Issuance of Leases

The entire 5-year program process takes approximately two years to complete. The lease sale schedule is reviewed annually after its approval. A more in-depth discussion of the leasing process is provided in MMS's document, *Leasing Oil and Gas Resources: Outer Continental Shelf*. The document is available through MMS's website at www.mms.gov/ld/PDFs/GreenBook-LeasingDocument.pdf.

The MMS has begun its proposed OCS Oil and Gas Leasing Program for 2007-2012. The 5-Year Program proposes 11 oil and gas lease sales in the GOM—5 sales in the WPA and 6 sales in the CPA. More information on the 5-Year Program may be gleaned from the following MMS's website at http://www.mms.gov/5-year/WhatIs5YearProgram.htm.

The GOM Outer Continental Shelf is divided into the three sectors—the Western, Central, and Eastern Planning Areas (**Figure 11**). This figure displays the reconfigured administrative planning area boundaries designated by MMS (*Federal Register*, 2006). Sale 204, held on August 22, 2007, was the first offering in the current 5-Year Program that utilized these new boundaries. Note that data in this report prior to July 1, 2007, use the old planning area delineations.

WATER-DEPTH INTERVALS

Many of the data presented in this report are subdivided according to water depth. These divisions (1,000, 1,500, 5,000, and 7,500 ft) are illustrated in **Figure 11**, along with the deepwater royalty-relief zones (400, 800, 1,600, and 2,000 m) mandated by the Energy Policy Act of 2005. Royalty-relief volumes were changed with the passage of this Act. Not all leases within a colored area are eligible for royalty relief because of the differing vintage of leases included within the area.

LEASING ACTIVITY

Figure 12 depicts all active leases in the GOM at the end of calendar year 2007. The pie chart inset in this figure highlights the relative percentage of active leases in each operational water-depth category used in this report. Note that approximately 54 percent of the leased blocks are located in water depths greater than 1,000 ft (305 m). The limited number of active leases in the EPA is related to leasing restrictions. The approximate number of active leases for certain water-depth ranges is shown in **Table 3**.

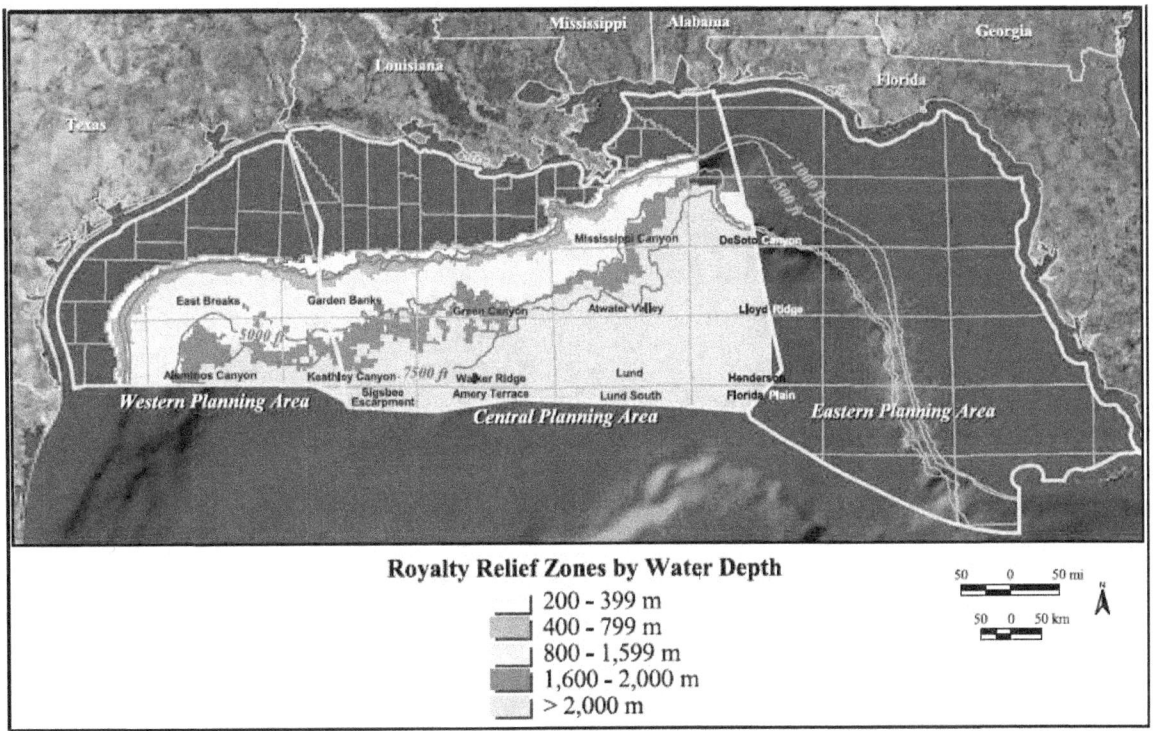

Figure 11. Deepwater royalty-relief zones with planning areas and selected bathymetry.

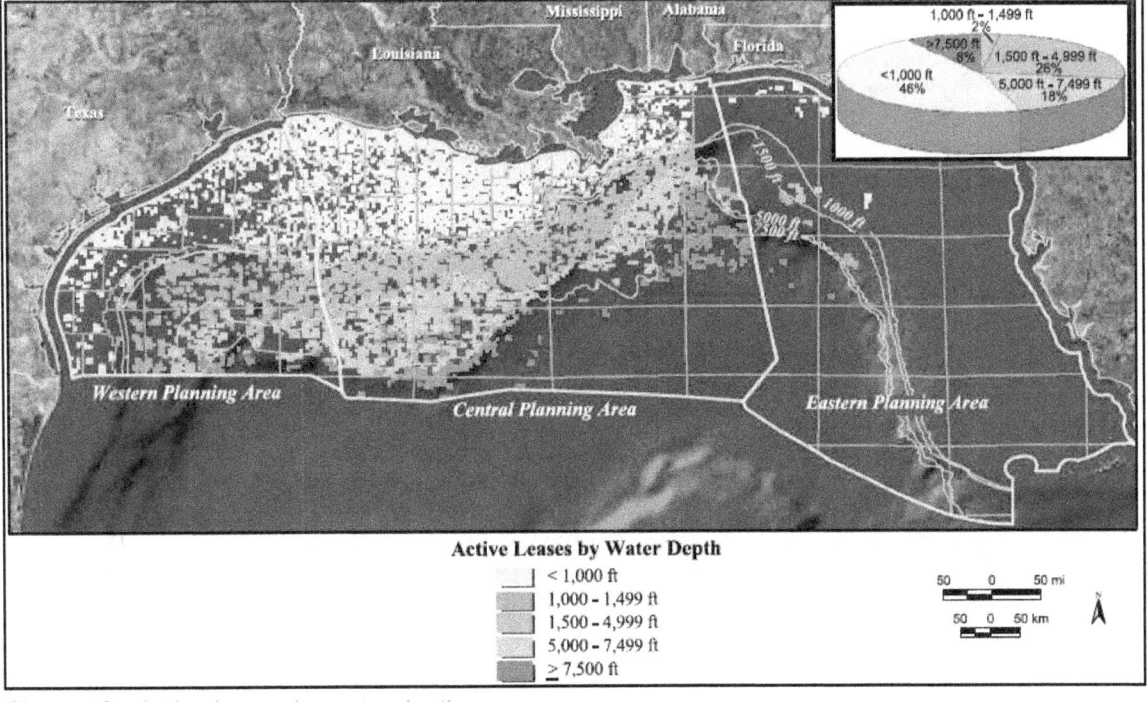

Figure 12. Active leases by water depth.

Table 3. Number of Active Leases by Water-Depth Interval

Number of Active Leases	Water Depth	
	ft	m
3,409	<1,000	<305
164	1,000-1,499	305-457
1,912	1,500-4,999	457-1,524
1,319	5,000-7,499	1,524-2,286
639	>7,500	>2,286

Data compiled as of 12/31/2007.

2007 LEASE SALES

In 2007, two lease sales were held—Sale 204 (WPA, on August 22) and Sale 205 (CPA, on October 3). These were the first sales held under the revised planning area boundaries of the GOM. Together the two 2007 sales amassed approximately $3.2 billion in high bids and about $5.6 billion for all bids received, resulting in the issuance of 956 leases.

Sale 204 garnered approximately $290 million in high bids on 282 blocks and about $370 million for all 358 bids received for the sale. Slightly over 64 percent of the bids were for blocks in water depths of 800 m (2,625 ft) or greater. This interval also constituted over 85 percent of the high bids for this sale. The water-depth interval of 800 m to less than 1,600 m (2,625 ft to less than 5,249 ft) amassed the most number of high bids (108) in the sale. Over 52 percent of the high bids were for blocks in water depths of 1,600 m (5,249 ft) or more. The MMS considers this interval as ultra-deep water. Sale 204 ultimately resulted in the award of 274 leases. Eight high bids were rejected by MMS. The accepted high bids for the sale totaled about $287 million.

Sale 205 was an exceptional lease offering that attracted over $2.9 billion in high bids on 723 blocks – the third largest total in U.S. leasing history. Only Sale 72 (held in 1983, with approximately $3.5 billion in high bids) and Sale 206 (held in 2008, with approximately $3.7 billion in high bids) exceeded the level of interest for Sale 205. The sum of all 1,428 bids for Sale 205 was approximately $5.25 billion.

About 66 percent of the high bids in Sale 205 were for blocks in water depths of 800 m (2,625 ft) or greater. Over 89 percent of the high bid sum for this sale was offered for blocks in this water depth range. Approximately 40 percent of the high bids in this sale were in ultra-deep water. Clearly, deep water played a major part in this sale. Ultimately, the bids on 682 blocks were deemed acceptable by MMS. The bids on 18 blocks were rejected and bids on 23 blocks were forfeited by the high bidders. The accepted high bids for the sale totaled approximately $2.8 billion.

The success of Sale 205 was influenced by the reconfiguration of the planning areas (**Figure 13**). Acreage lost in the WPA and EPA was incorporated into the CPA. For leases in deep water, 37 percent are attributed to these gained areas. High bids on these leases totaled $974.2 million.

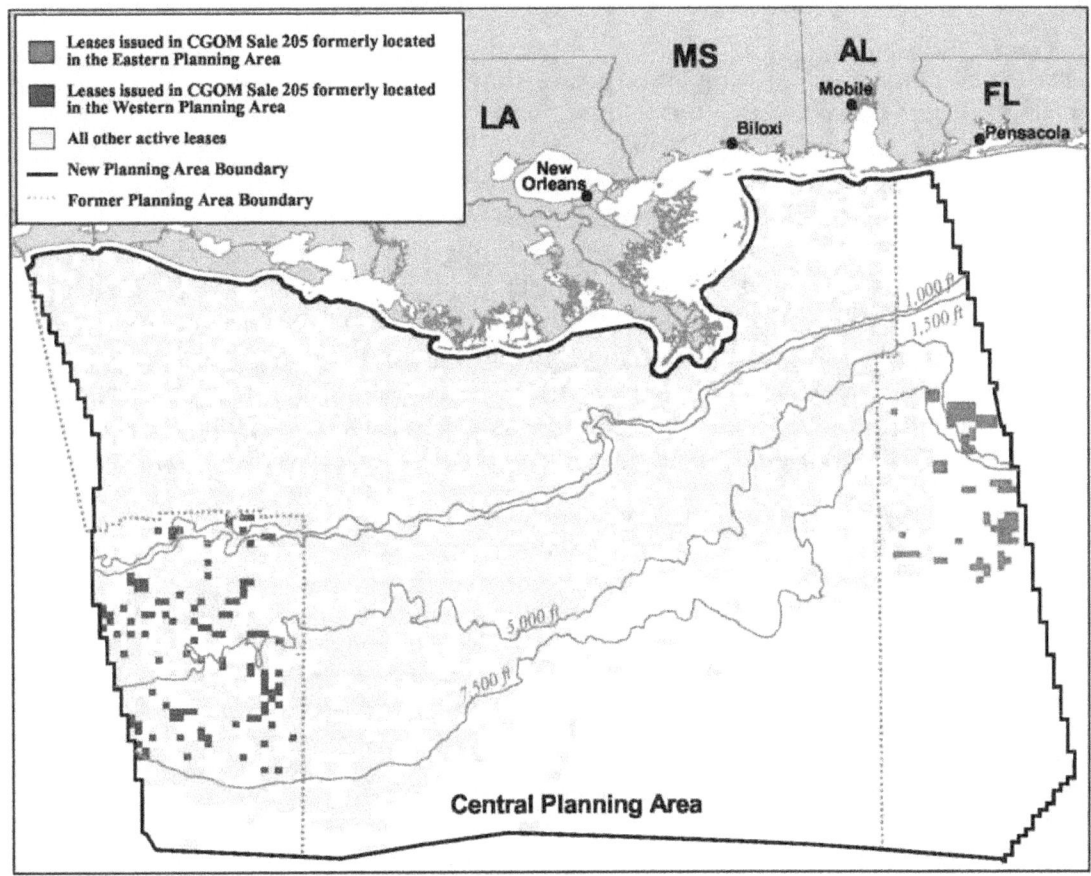

Figure 13. Comparison of planning area changes.

2008 LEASE SALES

This year saw a record-setting lease sale. Sale 206, a CPA offering, was held on March 19. This sale attracted approximately $3.7 billion in high bids – the most since Federal offshore leasing began in 1954. The MMS received 1,057 bids from 85 companies on 615 blocks. The sum of all bids for this sale was approximately $5.7 billion. About 67 percent of the blocks receiving bids were located in deep water [1,312 ft (400 m) or deeper] with approximately 34 percent of the tracts bid upon in ultra-deep water – more than 5,249 ft (1,600 m).[1] The sum of the high bids for deepwater tracts was 93.2 percent of the total. The ultra-deepwater high bids accounted for 54.1 percent of the total high bids.

The EPA Sale 224 was held on the same day as Sale 206. The MMS received 58 bids from 6 companies on 36 blocks resulting in about $64.7 million in high bids. The sum of all bids received was approximately $72.1 million. All of the blocks receiving bids are located in water depths of greater than 2,625 ft (800 m). An estimated 37.5 percent of the high bid amount from the sale will go directly to four Gulf producing States. Sale 224 was the first sale where sharing provisions of the Gulf of Mexico Energy Security Act of 2006 will start immediately.

---

[1] The definitions of deep water and ultra-deep water used here are based on the DWRRA established royalty suspension intervals.

LEASING TRENDS

Prior to the mid-1990's, leasing activities in the GOM were concentrated in the shallow-water blocks located on the continental shelf [water depths of approximately 200 m (656 ft)] or less. With the passage of the DWRRA in 1995, royalty-relief incentives were established for new leases on the basis of specific water-depth intervals. The water-depth categories depicted in **Figure 14** reflect the divisions used in the DWRRA. This figure shows the magnitude of the DWRRA's impact on leasing activities. Significant deepwater leasing activities began in 1995 and showed remarkable increases from 1996 through 1998, especially in the water depths of greater than 800 m (2,625 ft), where the greatest royalty relief was available. During this time, leasing activities on shallow-water blocks diminished. The number of leases issued in the greater than 800-m water depth interval slightly increased from 1999 to 2003, then leveled off until 2005. However, from 2006 to 2007, a 66 percent increase occurred in the number of leases issued in this water-depth range.

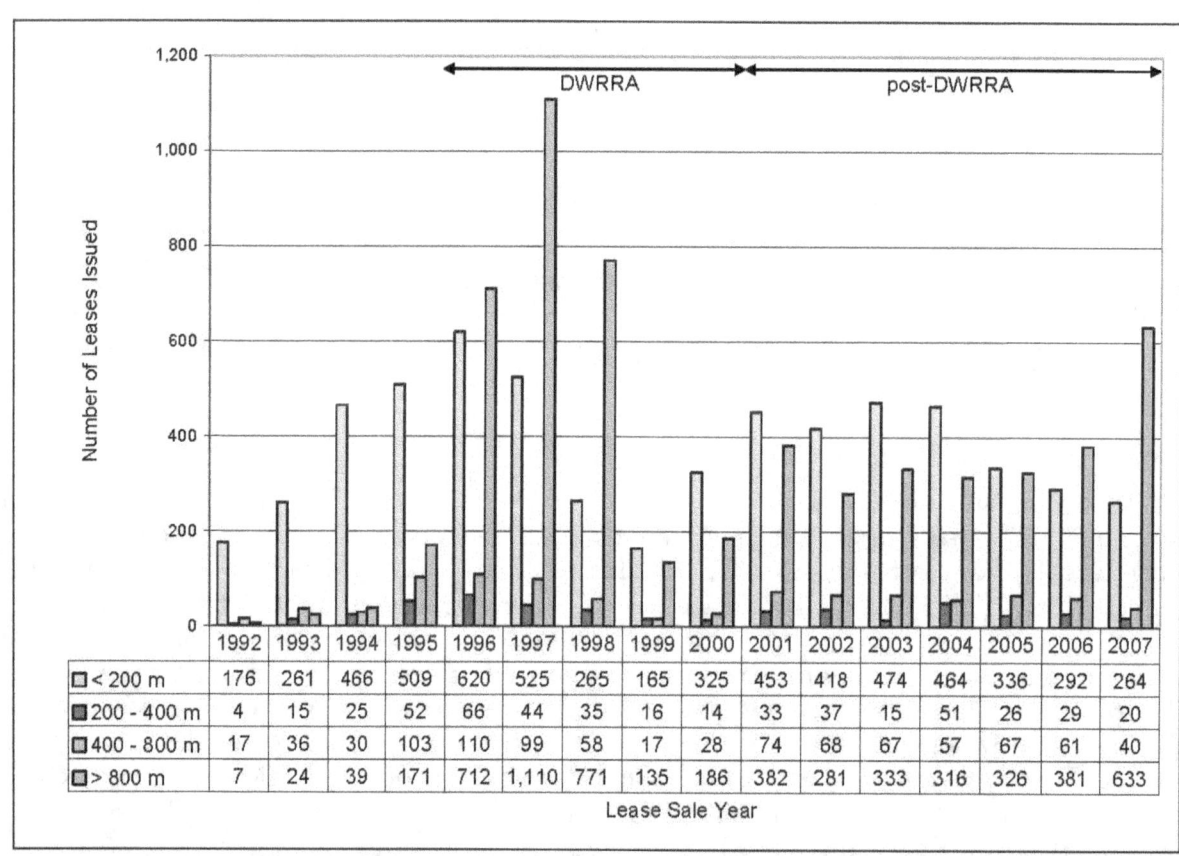

	1992	1993	1994	1995	1996	1997	1998	1999	2000	2001	2002	2003	2004	2005	2006	2007
< 200 m	176	261	466	509	620	525	265	165	325	453	418	474	464	336	292	264
200 - 400 m	4	15	25	52	66	44	35	16	14	33	37	15	51	26	29	20
400 - 800 m	17	36	30	103	110	99	58	17	28	74	68	67	57	67	61	40
> 800 m	7	24	39	171	712	1,110	771	135	186	382	281	333	316	326	381	633

Lease Sale Year

Figure 14. Number of leases issued each year, subdivided by DWRRA water-depth categories.

Figure 15 was derived from the data in **Figure 14**, but displays the deepwater depth categories used elsewhere in this report. (Shallow-water data are excluded from **Figure 15**.)

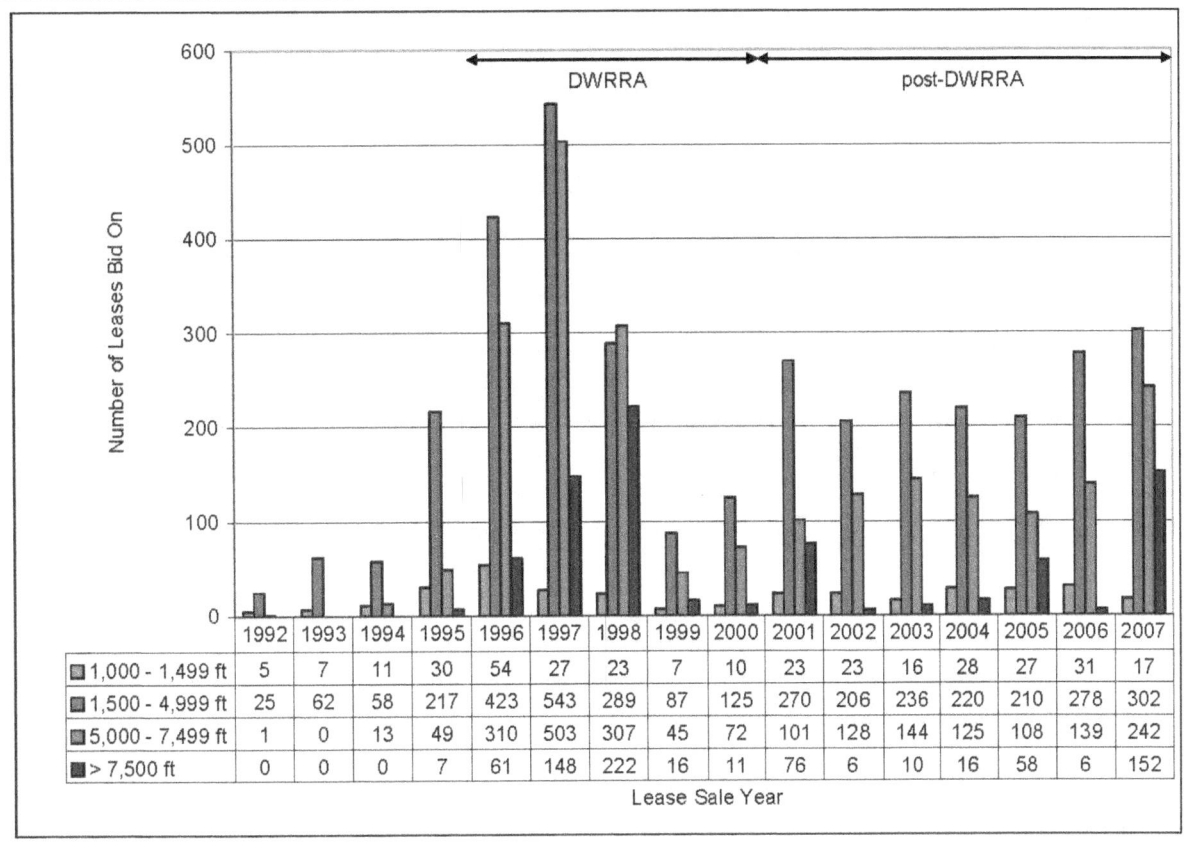

	1992	1993	1994	1995	1996	1997	1998	1999	2000	2001	2002	2003	2004	2005	2006	2007
◼ 1,000 - 1,499 ft	5	7	11	30	54	27	23	7	10	23	23	16	28	27	31	17
◼ 1,500 - 4,999 ft	25	62	58	217	423	543	289	87	125	270	206	236	220	210	278	302
◼ 5,000 - 7,499 ft	1	0	13	49	310	503	307	45	72	101	128	144	125	108	139	242
◼ > 7,500 ft	0	0	0	7	61	148	222	16	11	76	6	10	16	58	6	152

Lease Sale Year

Figure 15. Number of leases bid on for each deepwater interval.

These deepwater data show the rapid increase in leasing activity that began in 1995 and continued through 1998. Although leasing activity plummeted in 1999, higher levels of leasing activity returned after 2000. Several factors initiated this resurgence, including high oil and gas prices and several major discoveries, such as Mad Dog and Thunder Horse.

Beginning in 1999, the 1,500-4,999 ft (457-1,524 m) and 5,000-7,499 ft (1,524-2,286 m) intervals generally parallel each other, with the 1,500-4,999 ft (457-1524 m) outpacing the deeper water range. Through 2003, the ranges steadily increased, then leveled off in 2004 and 2005, and from 2006 to the present, both intervals steadily increased. An astronomical jump occurred from 2006 to 2007 in the greater than 7,500-ft (2,286-m) depth category – from 6 to 152 for the number of blocks bid on.

LEASE OWNERSHIP

Major oil and gas companies (BP, ChevronTexaco, ExxonMobil, and Shell) blazed the trail into deep water in the 1980's and early 1990's. **Figure 16** illustrates the relative leaseholding positions of majors versus nonmajors (as of December 31, 2007). Nonmajors began acquiring significant leaseholdings in the mid-1990's, a trend that continued through 2007. In fact, the pie chart in **Figure 16** shows that nonmajors now hold over 66 percent of all of the deepwater leases.

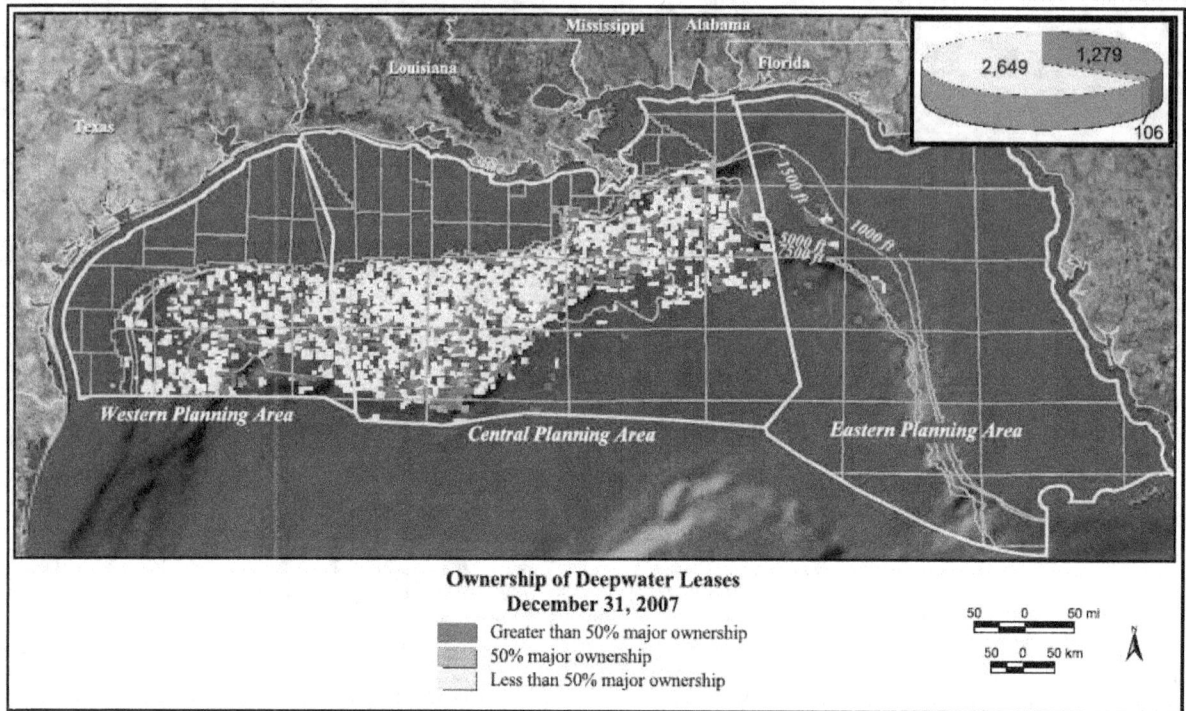

Figure 16. Ownership of deepwater leases.

FUTURE LEASE ACTIVITY

The number of leases that will be relinquished, terminated, or expire will influence activity in future lease sales. Given the fact that most companies can drill only a small percentage of their active leases, it is likely that many high-quality leases will expire without being tested. Ultimately, an untested and undeveloped lease will expire and possibly be leased again.

The deepwater arena in the GOM experienced phenomenal leasing activities from 1996 through 1998. This is especially noticeable in the greater than 800-m (2,625-ft) water depth range. During this time, this interval constituted about 47 percent (1996) and 62 percent (1997) of the total number of leases awarded from each year's lease sales. In the 2006 and 2007 sales, about 40 percent of the total number of leases issued in water depths greater than 800 m (2,625 ft) was leases that were expired, terminated, or relinquished from the 1996 and 1997 sales.

Figure 17 shows leases that may expire from 2009 to 2018 in two-year intervals. The data used in creating these figures assume that each lease expires at the end of its primary lease term (without a lease-term extension). Note that lease terms vary according to water depth. Primary lease terms for the following water depth intervals are: 5 years for blocks in less than 400 m (1,312 ft), 8 years for blocks in 400-799 m (1,312-2,621 ft) (pursuant to 30 CFR 256.37, commencement of an exploratory well is required within the first 5 years of the initial 8-year term to avoid lease cancellation), and 10 years for blocks in 800 m (2,625 ft) or greater. **Appendix B** provides a chronological listing of all GOM lease offerings arranged by sale number, location, and date.

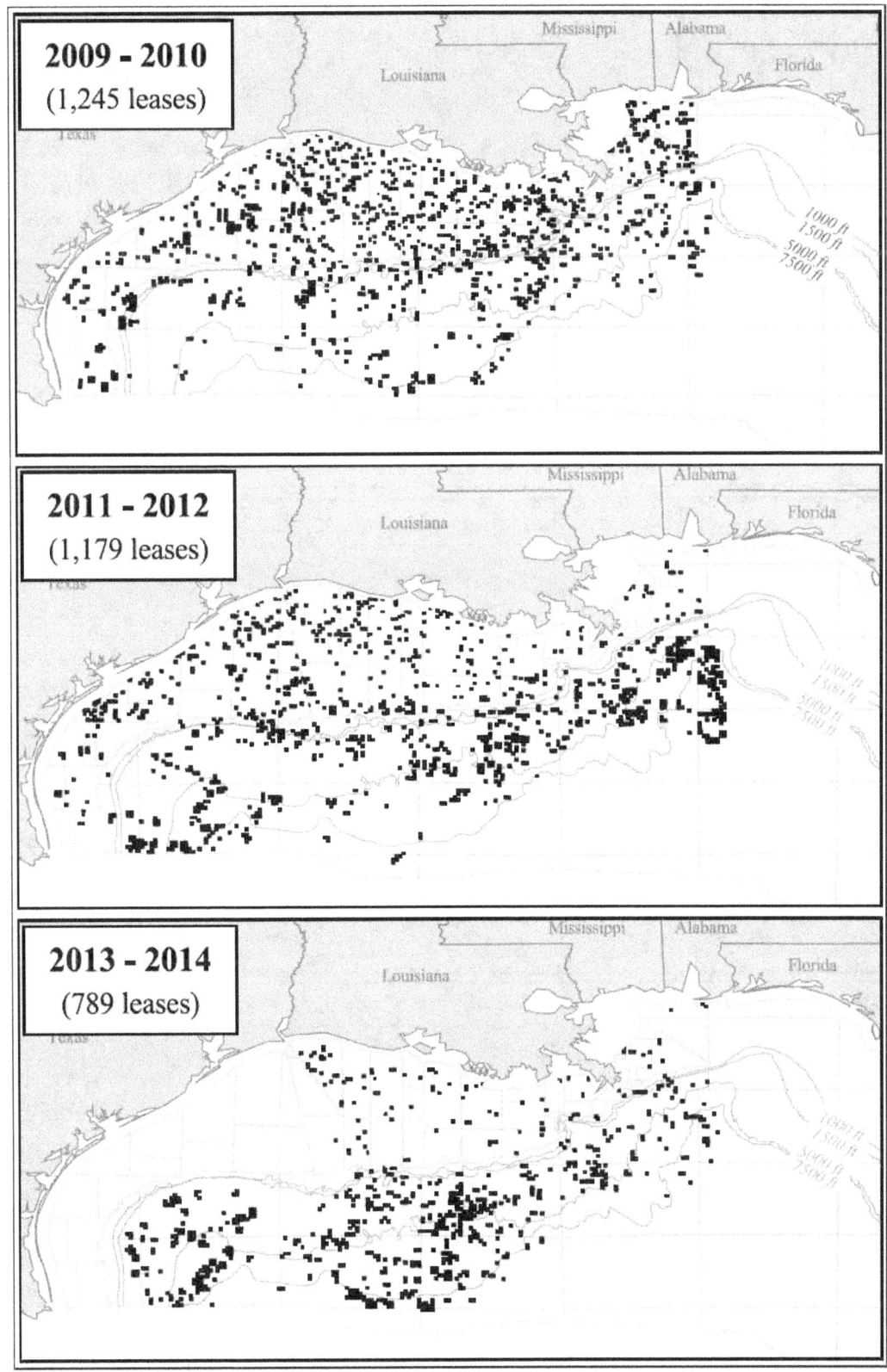

Figure 17. Anticipated lease expirations from 2009 to 2018.

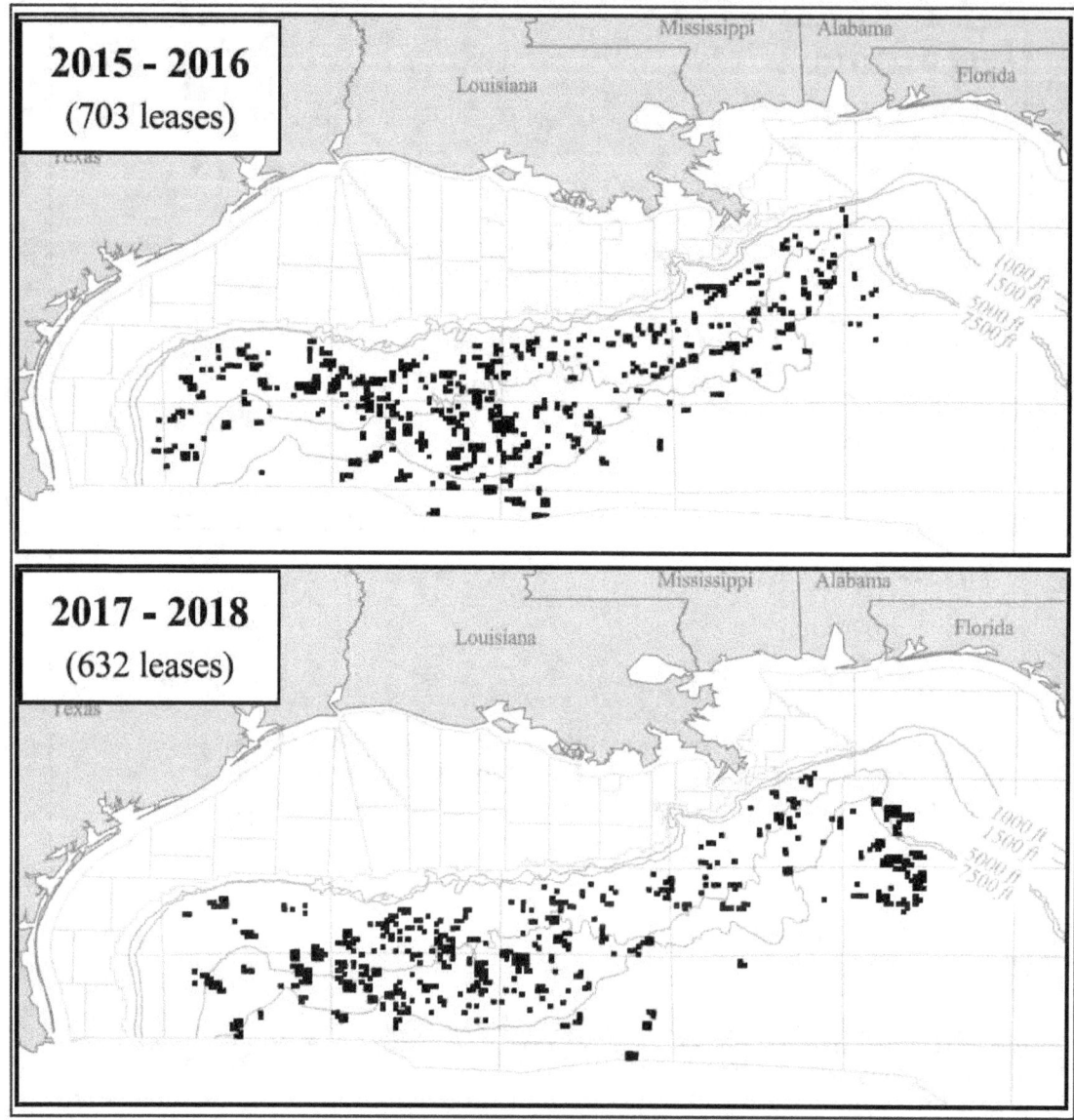

Figure 17. Anticipated lease expirations from 2009 to 2018 (*continued*).

ROYALTY AND RENTAL RATE INCREASES

On January 9, 2007, the Secretary of the Department of the Interior, Dirk Kempthorne, announced an increase in the royalty rate for new offshore deepwater Federal oil and gas leases (Kempthorne, 2007). The royalty rate was increased to 16.7 percent from the previous rate of 12.5 percent. This rate change took effect with the first GOM lease sale in 2007 – Sale 204 in the WPA.

On February 13, 2008, the Final Notices of Sale (73 FR 30) for Lease Sales 206 and 224, which were held consecutively on March 19, 2008, in the CPA and the EPA, respectively, included an increase in the royalty rate for deepwater leases to 18.75 percent from the 16.7 percent rate. The Notices also included changes to rental rates of $6.25 per acre for blocks in water depths of less than 200 m (656 ft) and $9.50 per acre for blocks in water depths of

200 m (656 ft) or deeper with a possible escalation in the rate if the lease has an approved extension of the initial 5-year period.

ROYALTY RELIEF

Deepwater royalty relief is available in Sale 206. A lease in water depths of 400 m (656 ft) or more will receive a royalty suspension according to the water-depth range in which the lease is located (**Table 4**).

Table 4. Royalty Relief for Sale 206

Water-Depth Range (m)	Royalty Suspension Amount (BOE[1])
400 to <800	5 million
800 to <1,600	9 million
1,600 to 2,000	12 million
>2,000	16 million

[1] Barrels of Oil Equivalent

There were price thresholds established for this sale above which the relief would end. The price thresholds are $35.75 per barrel of oil and $4.47 per Mcf of natural gas; both are based on 2006 dollars. The Final Notice of Sale for Sale 224 states there will be no Royalty Suspension Provisions offered for the resulting leases.

ENVIRONMENTAL ISSUES

Ocean Current Monitoring

The most energetic currents in the Gulf of Mexico affect the ocean from its surface down to approximately the 3,281-ft (1,000-m) water-depth level with varying speeds. Currents as high as 4 knots (kn) [4.6 miles per hour (mph)] have been observed from the surface to 1,000-ft (305-m) water depths. These upper currents taper off between 1,000- and 3,281-ft (305- and 1,000-m) depths.

Beneath the 3,281-ft (1,000-m) water-depth level, other currents migrate around the deep waters of the GOM. These deep currents were once thought to be minimal and were not a major consideration in most structure designs. In 1999, industry reported significant currents below 3,000 ft (914 m). This information led to a Safety Alert (USDOI, MMS, 2000; Notice No. 180) and subsequent studies of deep currents by MMS (Hamilton et al., 2003 and 2000). These studies revealed significant deep currents of up to 2 kn (2.3 mph) at some locations. The Hamilton et al. investigations spawned another deepwater current study funded by MMS—the "Exploratory Study of Deepwater Currents in the Gulf of Mexico" (Donohue et al., 2006a and 2006b).

The latest physical oceanographic study, "Full-Water Column Current Observations in the Central Gulf of Mexico" (Sheinbaum et al., 2007) provides more insight into the Gulf's currents. Perhaps the most remarkable finding of this study is that the data suggest highly coherent motions throughout the water column, which largely decompose into barotropic and first baroclinic mode structures. Progressive vector diagrams and vector plots suggest an upper layer from the surface down to the 2,625-2,953 ft (800-900 m) depth, a transition layer between 2,953-3,937 ft (900-1,200 m), more in tune with the upper layer, and a deep coherent layer below 3,937 ft (1,200 m). This partition is consistent with the thermodynamic studies of Rivas et al. (2005 and in review) and the analysis of the deep circulation in the Caribbean and Gulf of Mexico of Sturges (2005). The highly coherent motions below 3,281 ft (1,000 m), their bottom intensification, and their spectral characteristics are definitely reminiscent of topographic Rossby wave motions, as reported by Hamilton et al. (2003). Additional information is available on MMS's website at http://www.gomr.mms.gov/homepg/regulate/environ/techsumm/rec_pubs.html.

Incidents have occurred in the deepwater areas of the Gulf that demonstrate the need for more accurate data in hindcasting and forecasting events and in daily operations. The MMS issued the Notice to Lessees and Operators (NTL) 2007-G17, "Deepwater Ocean Current Monitoring on Floating Facilities," in May 2007 (USDOI, MMS, 2007), which superseded NTL 2005-G02. The NTL implemented a program where operators of deepwater offshore production facilities and mobile offshore drilling units (MODU's) collect data on ocean currents and submit them to the National Oceanic and Atmospheric Administration (NOAA), which makes these data available to the general public on their Internet website at http://www.ndbc.noaa.gov/maps/ADCP_WestGulf.shtml. Data collected on currents may improve fatigue forecast models and help establish responsible design criteria, resulting in increased reliability of deepwater structures, thereby reducing risk to human lives, offshore facilities, and the ocean environment.

Deepwater Shipwrecks

Oil and gas industry activities on the seafloor in deep water (>1,000 ft or >305 m) have yielded an unexpected cultural resource bounty in the form of well-preserved historic shipwrecks relating to America's maritime past. Initial discoveries came as a result of high-resolution sonar surveys along pipeline rights-of-way in Mississippi Canyon. The MMS requirement for high-resolution sonar surveys of lease blocks was typically waived in deep water, allowing companies to substitute 3-D seismic data for their hazards analyses. Several important discoveries were made from these pipeline surveys, including the remains of the German submarine U-166, the only U-boat lost in the northern Gulf of Mexico (http://www.pastfoundation.org/U166/). As a result of a growing inventory of shipwrecks discovered along pipeline routes, MMS issued NTL 2006-G07, which expanded the area requiring archaeological surveys to include all of Mississippi Canyon and parts of Green Canyon, Ewing Bank, and Viosca Knoll. Of the 27 shipwrecks discovered in deep water, 11 were reported since this NTL went into effect.

Some of the deepwater shipwreck discoveries were casualties of World War II submarine attacks. In addition to the U-166 mentioned above, the freighter *Alcoa Puritan*, the passenger steamer *Robert E. Lee*, and the oil tankers *GulfPenn* and *GulfOil* are among the ships located in water depths of up to 6,500 ft (1,981 m). A recent study conducted by MMS found that, besides their historical interest, the wrecks had become thriving biological communities; the *GulfPenn* in particular is hosting dense colonies of *Lophelia* coral (http://www.pastfoundation.org/DeepWrecks/ and Church et al., 2007).

Nineteenth-century sailing vessels are also well represented among the inventory of deepwater shipwrecks. Unfortunately, of the five known 19th-century wrecks, three were impacted to some degree as a result of industry activities. One of these, dubbed the Mardi Gras Shipwreck that was named after the pipeline where it was discovered, was the subject of a mitigative data recovery operation in 2007 (http://www.flpublicarchaeology.org/mardigras/). Another 19th-century wreck was discovered in a pipeline post-lay survey – the pipeline was laid directly across it (Atauz et al., 2006). Although a survey was conducted of the pipeline route, the shipwreck fell in the nadir between the left and right sonar channels, and its location was inadvertently missed in the analysis. The MMS has subsequently required an offset survey line to ensure complete coverage of the proposed route's centerline. A third wooden-hulled wreck was discovered by a pipeline survey near a major offshore platform. The pipeline survey was conducted several years after the structure was installed. Subsequent investigations showed that a cable from an anchor of the drilling rig that was used during exploration or development activities had sliced through the stern portion of what appears to be a two-masted brig dating from the first quarter of the 19th century. The rig's anchor narrowly missed this historic vessel, which emphasizes the importance of conducting pre-disturbance seafloor surveys.

Several other shipwrecks have been detected by remote-sensing survey techniques. Their age, cultural affiliation, and historic significance remain unknown. The current MMS policy mandates that operators must avoid impacts to such potential cultural resources. It does not require operators to visually inspect or to identify them unless the company's proposed activities are likely to adversely affect the site. Since under Federal law the U.S. Government is not given title to shipwrecks outside State territorial waters, there is no requirement nor budget for MMS to investigate and inventory these potential resources. It is highly likely, however, that more sites will be located as industry moves into ever deeper water. Recent research suggests that the deepwater portions of the U.S. Exclusive Economic Zone (EEZ) were regularly traversed by ships as early as the 16th century, ships that were taking advantage of prevailing currents and winds, rather than hugging the coast as was long believed by historians (Lugo-Fernández et al., 2007). Inevitably, ships were lost along these deepwater routes as a result of storms, fires, acts of war, or a myriad of other causes and today remain like time capsules lying at the bottom of the Gulf.

Grid Programmatic Environmental Assessments

A biologically based grid system was developed by MMS as part of its comprehensive strategy to address deepwater issues. The grid system initially divided the Gulf into 17 areas or "grids" of biological similarity (**Figure 18**). Later, another grid was added to the system to address the modified Sale 181 Area, making a total of 18 grids for the Gulf.

Under this strategy, MMS will prepare a programmatic environmental assessment (PEA) that analyzes a proposed development project within each of the grids and that characterizes the whole grid. These grid PEA's are comprehensive in terms of the impact-producing factors and in terms of the environmental and socioeconomic resources described and analyzed for the entire grid. They also address potential cumulative effects of proposed projects within the grid. Other information on publicly announced projects within the grid is discussed, as well as any potential effects expected from future developmental activities. Projects selected for the PEA's are representative of the types of development expected for the grid. For example, a good candidate for a PEA would be a development plan that proposed a new structure that might serve as a "hub" for future developmental activities within the grid.

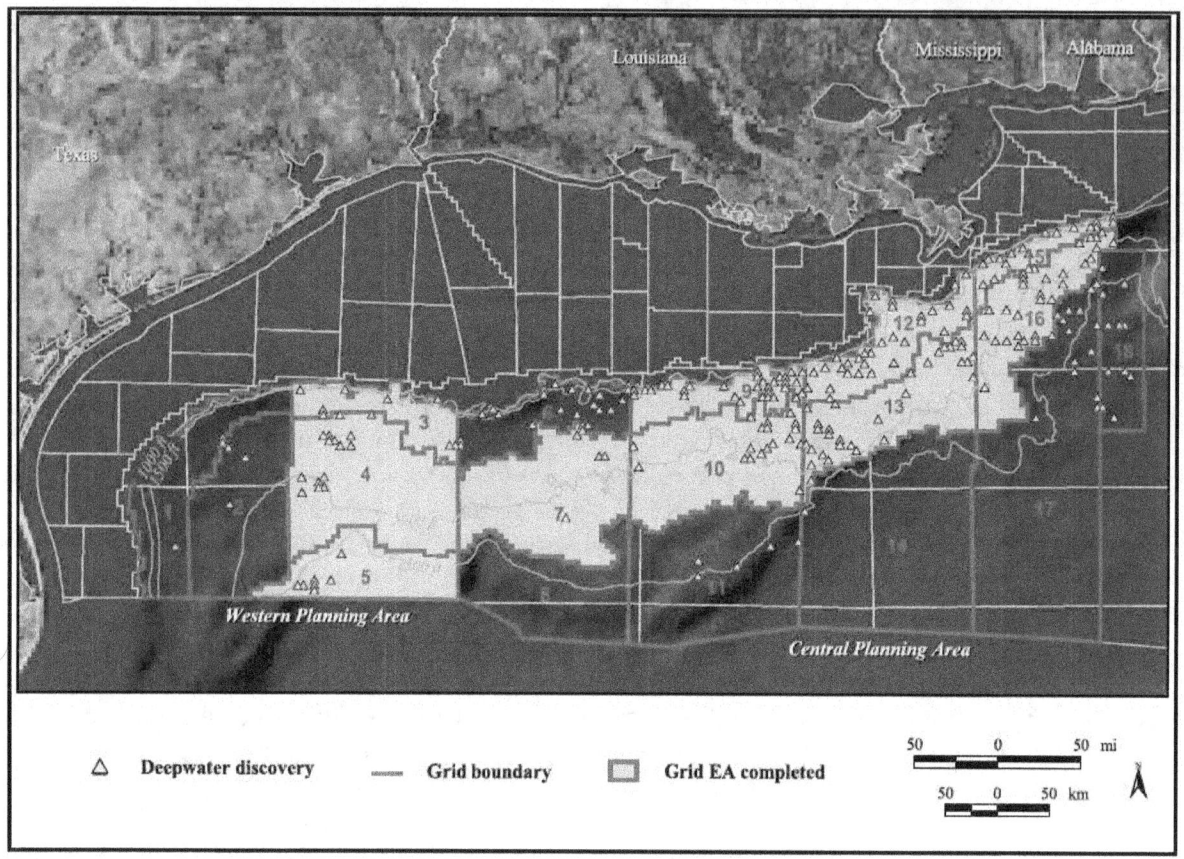

Figure 18. Grid PEA status.

Once a grid PEA has been completed, it will serve as a reference document to implement the "tiering" and "incorporation by reference" concepts detailed in the implementing regulations of NEPA. Future environmental evaluation documents may reference appropriate sections from these PEA's to reduce duplication of issues and effects in the documents that were appropriately addressed in the grid PEA's. This will allow the subsequent environmental analyses to focus on specific issues and effects related to the proposals being currently evaluated. **Table 5** provides specific information about the ten completed grid PEA's.

While the PEA's are generally prepared for developmental activities within the grid boundaries, MMS also foresaw the need to address proposed exploration activities in the EPA. A PEA was prepared that focused on Grid 18, the 256-block modified Sale 181 Area, and addressed only exploration activities in this sector of the Gulf. The document serves as a reference designed to streamline the processing of environmental evaluations required to assess industry exploration plans in this part of the EPA (USDOI, MMS, 2003).

Table 5. Grid PEA Status within the Central and Western Planning Areas

Grid	Project Name	Company	Plan	Area and Blocks
3	Gunnison	Kerr-McGee	N-7625	GB 667, 668, & 669
4	Nansen	Kerr-McGee	N-7045	EB 602 & 646
5	Perdido	Shell	N-8809	AC 812, 813, 814, & 857
7	Magnolia	Conoco	N-7506	GB 783 & 784
9	Phoenix	Energy Resource Technology	S-7156	GC 236 & 237
10	Holstein	British Petroleum	N-7216	GC 644 & 645
12	Medusa	Murphy	N-7269	MC 538 & 582
13	Marco Polo	Anadarko	N-7753	GC 608
15	Matterhorn	TotalFinaElf	N-7249	MC 243
16	Thunder Horse	British Petroleum	N-7469	MC 775-778 & 819-822

AC = Alaminos Canyon   EB = East Breaks   GB = Garden Banks
GC = Green Canyon   MC = Mississippi Canyon

DRILLING AND DEVELOPMENT

Deepwater drilling occurs from MODU's, such as semisubmersible units or drillships (**Figures 19** and **20**), and from stationary rigs located on combination production/drilling platforms (**Figure 21**). Numerous deepwater prospects are waiting to be drilled, and many may remain undrilled as the primary lease terms expire because of the limited number of rigs available for deepwater drilling in the GOM. In addition, the increased depths to which some operators are drilling cause rigs to be under contract for longer periods. Industry responded to the limited rig availability by ordering several new semisubmersibles in 2007. For example, ENSCO has four dynamically positioned semisubmersibles under construction and capable of drilling in 8,500 ft (2,591 m) of water. The first is expected to be completed in 2008; all four will be completed by 2010 (http://www.enscous.com). Additionally, PetroMENA ASA has three deepwater rigs under construction and capable of drilling in 10,000 ft (3,048 m) of water. The first two will be ready in 2009 and are contracted to Petrobras. The third rig will be ready in early 2010 and is contracted to Pemex (http://www.petrolia.no).

Figure 19. The *Deepwater Horizon*, a dynamically positioned, semisubmersible drilling unit (photo courtesy of Transocean).

Figure 20. The *Discoverer Enterprise*, a double-hulled, dynamically positioned drillship (photo courtesy of Transocean).

Figure 21. The *Thunder Horse* semisubmersible production facility (photo courtesy of BP).

Figure 22 depicts the maximum number of deepwater rigs operating in the GOM from 1992 through 2007.[2] After a peak in 2001, there was a small decline in rig availability through 2005. The number of rigs increased slightly in 2006 and has held steady through 2007. It is predicted that the number of rigs operating in intermediate water depths will decrease slightly in the coming years due to increased rig rates overseas. This will be offset by an increased number of rigs predicted to be capable of drilling in deep water.

Figure 23 shows the number of deepwater MODU's by water-depth categories in the GOM and worldwide. It can be seen that almost 43 percent of the rigs operating in the GOM are capable of drilling in water depths greater than 7,500 ft (2,286 m). Worldwide, the greatest number of rigs operate in the 1,500- to 4,999-ft (457- to 1,524-m) water depth range, with only 27 percent operating in water depths greater than 7,500 ft (2,286 m). Approximately 29 percent of the world's fleet of deepwater drilling rigs is committed to GOM service. The pie chart within **Figure 23** shows the distribution of deepwater rigs by major operating area. Most, if not all, of the deepwater-capable drilling rigs are under long-term contractual arrangements. The reader is cautioned not to draw conclusions from the rig count differences between **Figures 22 and 23**. **Figure 22** includes platform rigs in addition to MODU's; **Figure 23** addresses MODU's only. Further, not all MODU's in **Figure 23** are operating at any given time, and upgrades to MODU's that increase their water-depth capability will alter the maximum water depth rig counts shown; consequently, year-to-year comparisons may not be valid.

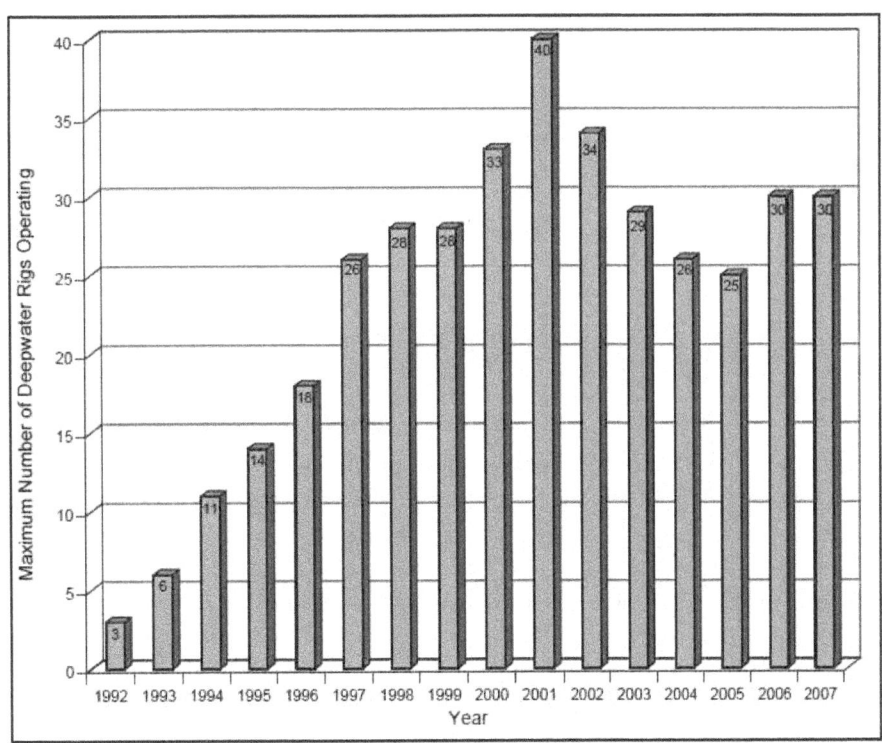

Figure 22. Maximum number of rigs operating in the deepwater Gulf of Mexico.

---

[2] It is important to note that the rig count includes platform rigs operating on deepwater production facilities in addition to the MODU's. The numbers do not distinguish between rigs drilling and those in service for completion and workover operations.

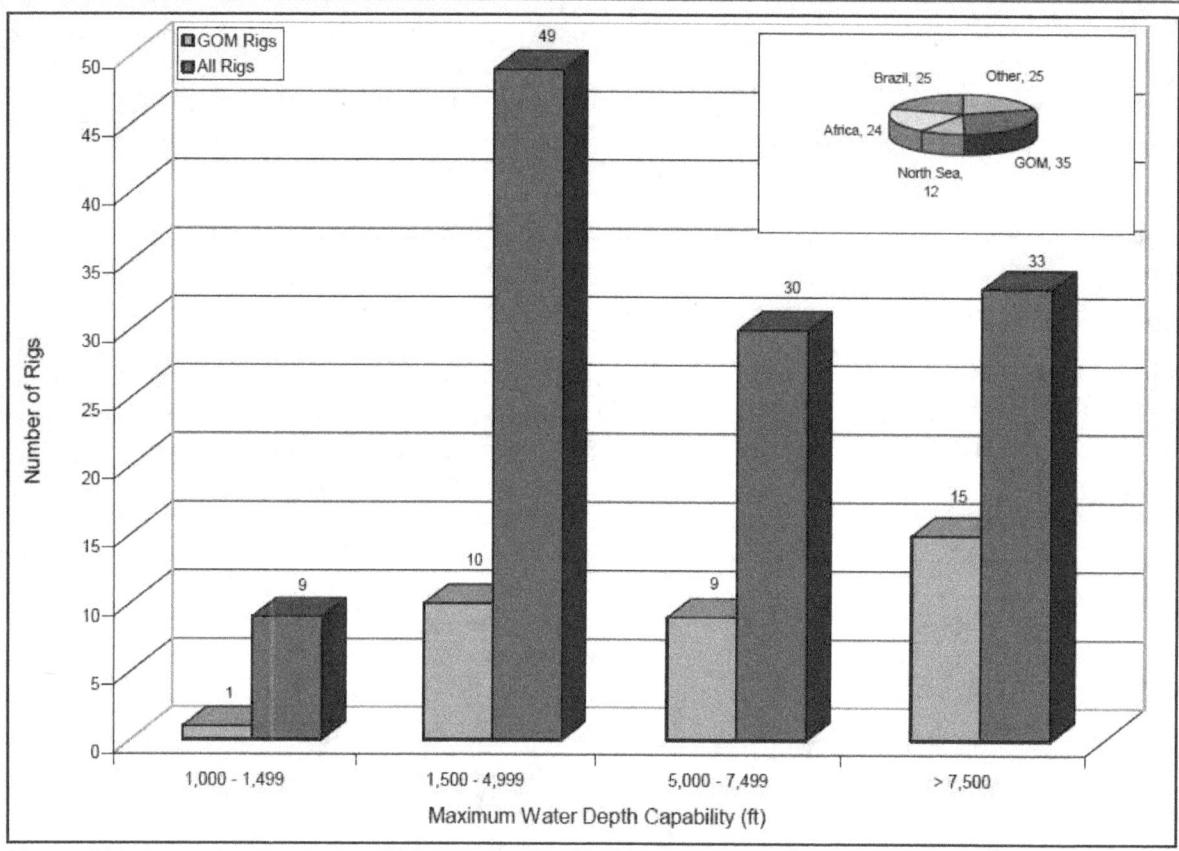

Figure 23. Approximate number of deepwater rigs (Gulf of Mexico and worldwide) subdivided according to their maximum water-depth capabilities. (Inset shows the number of deepwater rigs in various locations.)

DRILLING ACTIVITY

The number of deepwater wells drilled generally increased from 1992 through 2001 (**Figure 24**). Although there was a general decline from 2001 to 2004, the last three years have shown an upward trend. This figure shows that most of the drilling has occurred in the 1,500- to 4,999-ft (457- to 1,524-m) water-depth range. Only original boreholes and sidetracks are included in the well counts used in this report. Wells defined as "by-passes" are specifically excluded. A "by-pass" is a section of well that does not seek a new objective; it is intended to drill around a section of the wellbore made unusable by stuck pipe or equipment left in the wellbore.

Figures 25 and **26** break down the annual deepwater well counts (shown in **Figure 24**) into exploration and development wells, respectively. This report uses the designation of exploration and development wells provided by the operators. The data reflect the variations among operators in classifying wells as either exploration or development. After decreasing in 2002 and 2003, the number of exploration wells drilled increased through 2006 and slightly decreased in 2007. Exploratory drilling in the 1,500- to 4,999-ft (457- to 1,524-m) water-depth range remained the same from 2002 through 2004, but increased in 2005 and remained relatively level since then. From 2005 to 2006, the number of wells drilled in the 5,000- to 7,499-ft (1,524- to 2,286-m) water-depth range nearly doubled, and it has remained level through 2007. Overall, there has been a decrease in the number of development wells drilled from 2002 through 2005. Possible reasons for the decrease may be the method by which wells are categorized in this report (exploration versus development), the retention of exploration wells for production purposes, and the lag from exploration to first production. The complexity of developments in ultra-deep water may also be a factor, requiring operators to spend more time in planning and design. The total number of development wells has increased over the last 2 years. Remarkably, in 2007, 46 percent of the total number of development wells were drilled in the greater than 7,500-ft (2,286-m) water-depth interval. Almost all of these wells are associated with the Perdido Regional Development hub.

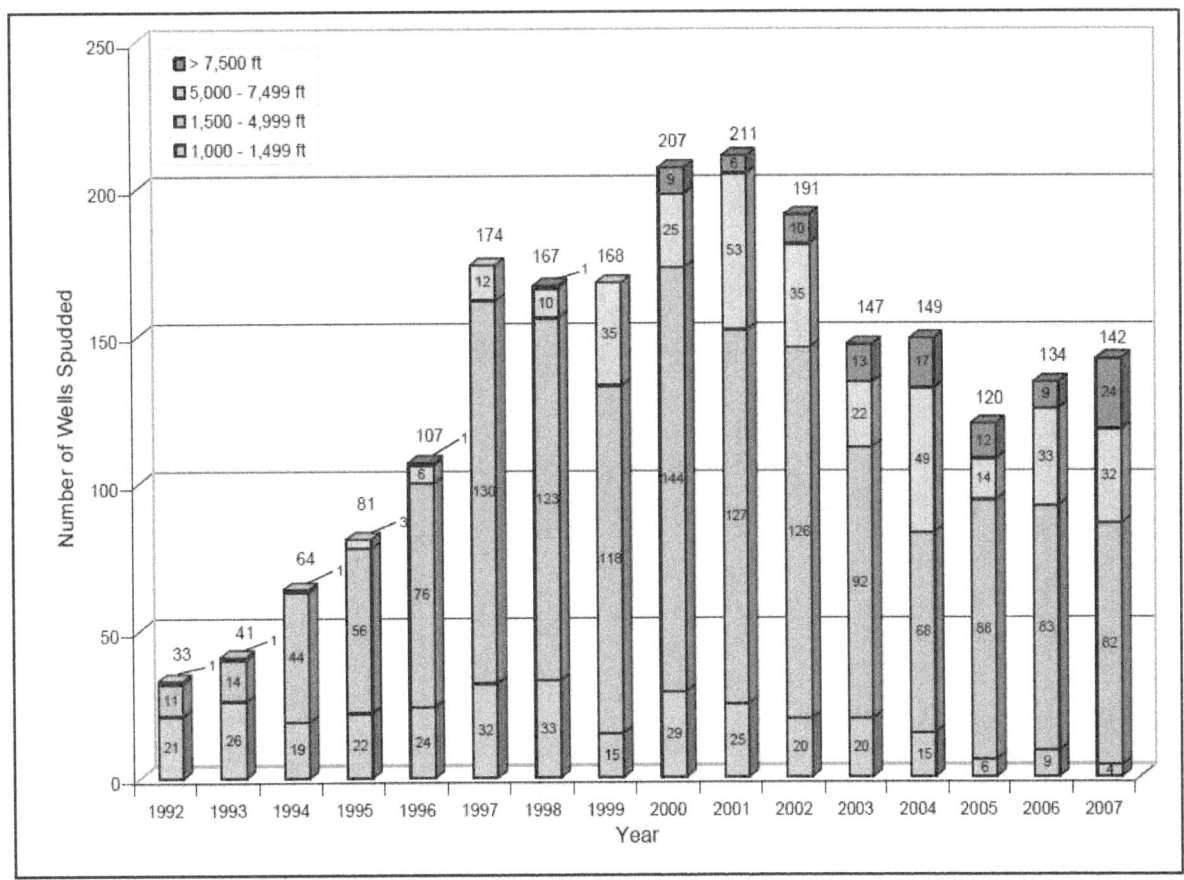

Figure 24. All deepwater wells drilled by water depth.

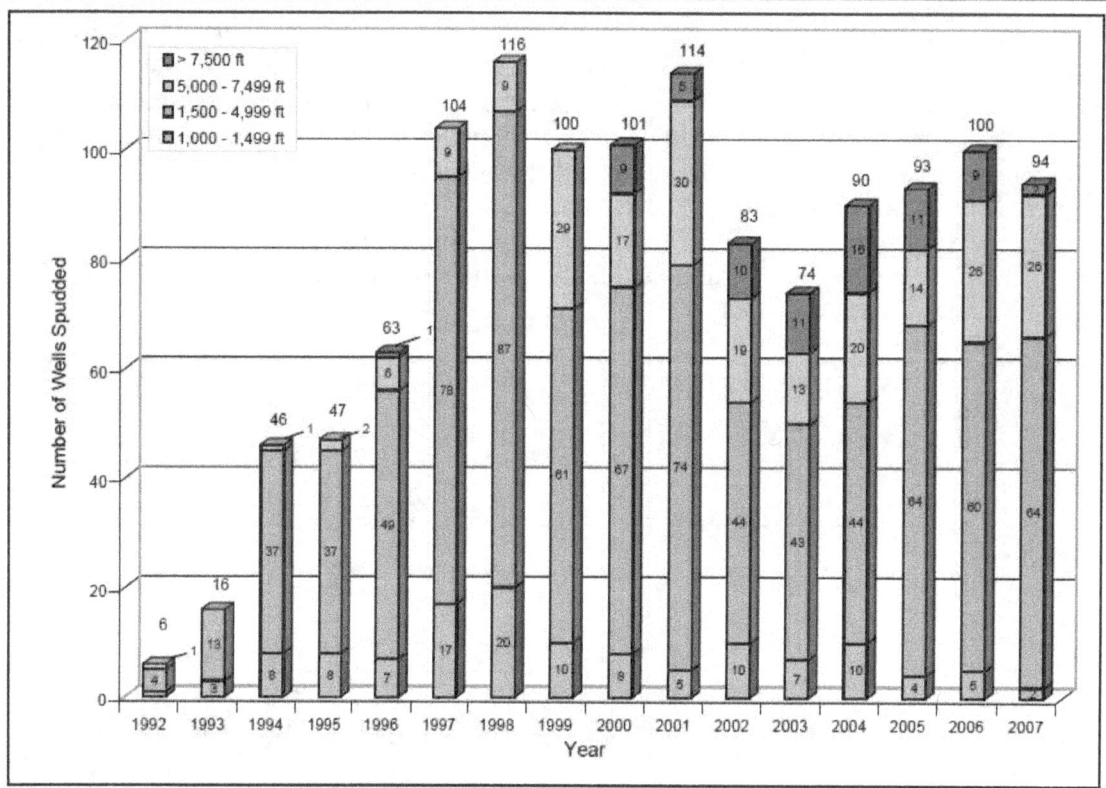

Figure 25. Deepwater exploration wells drilled by water depth.

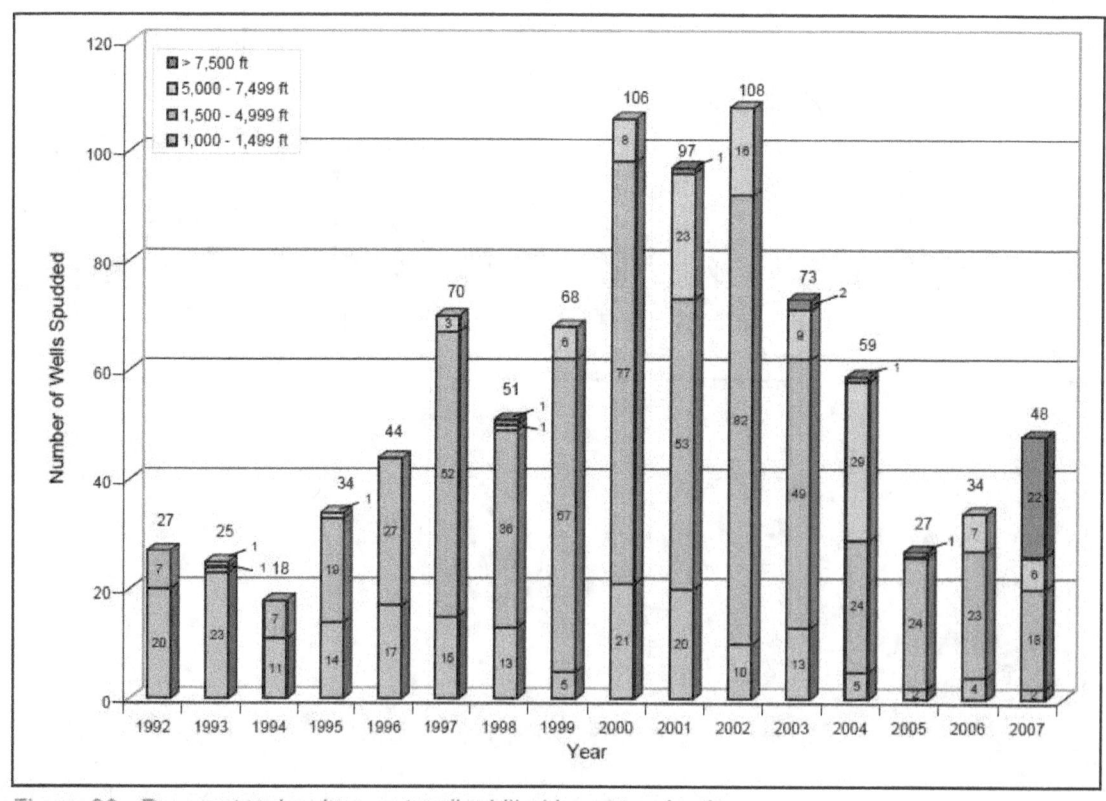

Figure 26. Deepwater development wells drilled by water depth.

Figure 27 illustrates the geographic distribution of deepwater exploration wells. Note the progression into deeper water through time. **Figure 28** depicts the locations of deepwater development wells. Once again, the data reveal a general increase in activity as well as a trend toward increasing water depth with time.

One indicator that MMS has found useful in projecting activity levels is the number of plans received. Although the order of plan submission and drilling activities can vary with projects, operators generally proceed as follows:

- file an Exploration Plan (EP),

- drill exploration wells,

- file a Conceptual Deep Water Operations Plan (CDWOP),

- file a Development Operations Coordination Document (DOCD),

- file a DWOP,

- drill development wells, then

- begin production.

Figure 29 shows the number of deepwater EP's, deepwater DOCD's, and DWOP's received each year since 1994 (DWOP's were not required until 1995). The count of EP's, DOCD's, and DWOP's includes only the initial plans. Some shallow-water activities are included in the DWOP data because DWOP's must be filed and approved for developments in greater than 1,000-ft (305-m) water depths and for all subsea developments regardless of water depth. The discussion of subsea wells later in this report will address the significance of shallow-water subsea tiebacks and the effective use of deepwater technologies in marginal developments.

There was a marked increase in EP's beginning in 1997. The number of EP's reached a peak of 92 in 1999, then hovered near 70 per year through 2005. Since then, EP submittals have declined. The number of DOCD submittals reached a high of 28 in 2005. Since then, the numbers have declined from that high, but have remained constant. The number of initial DWOP's has remained fairly consistent between 2000 and 2007 ranging from a low of 27 in 2007 and a high of 36 in 2001. The decrease in the number of plans received may be partially attributed to the complexities of activities associated with deep water, such as lack of rig availability, lack of infrastructure, and harsher operating environments.

Beginning in 1996, the maximum drilling depth increased rapidly, reaching depths below 30,000 ft (9,144 m) in 2002. The Transocean *Discoverer Spirit* drilled the deepest well in the GOM to date, Chevron/Unocal's Knotty Head discovery in Green Canyon Block 512, reaching a total vertical depth (TVD) of 34,158 ft (10,411 m) in December 2005. The recent dramatic increase in TVD may be attributed to several factors, including enhanced rig capabilities, deeper exploration targets, and the general trend toward greater water depths.

Chevron holds another world record—drilling in 10,011 ft (3,051 m) of water at its Toledo prospect in Alaminos Canyon Block 951 in November 2003. In 2006, a record was set for the deepest oil production test on Chevron's Jack prospect located in Walker Ridge Block 758. The Lower Tertiary Wilcox Formation was tested in the interval 26,739 to 27,292 ft (8,150 to 8,319 m) subsea.

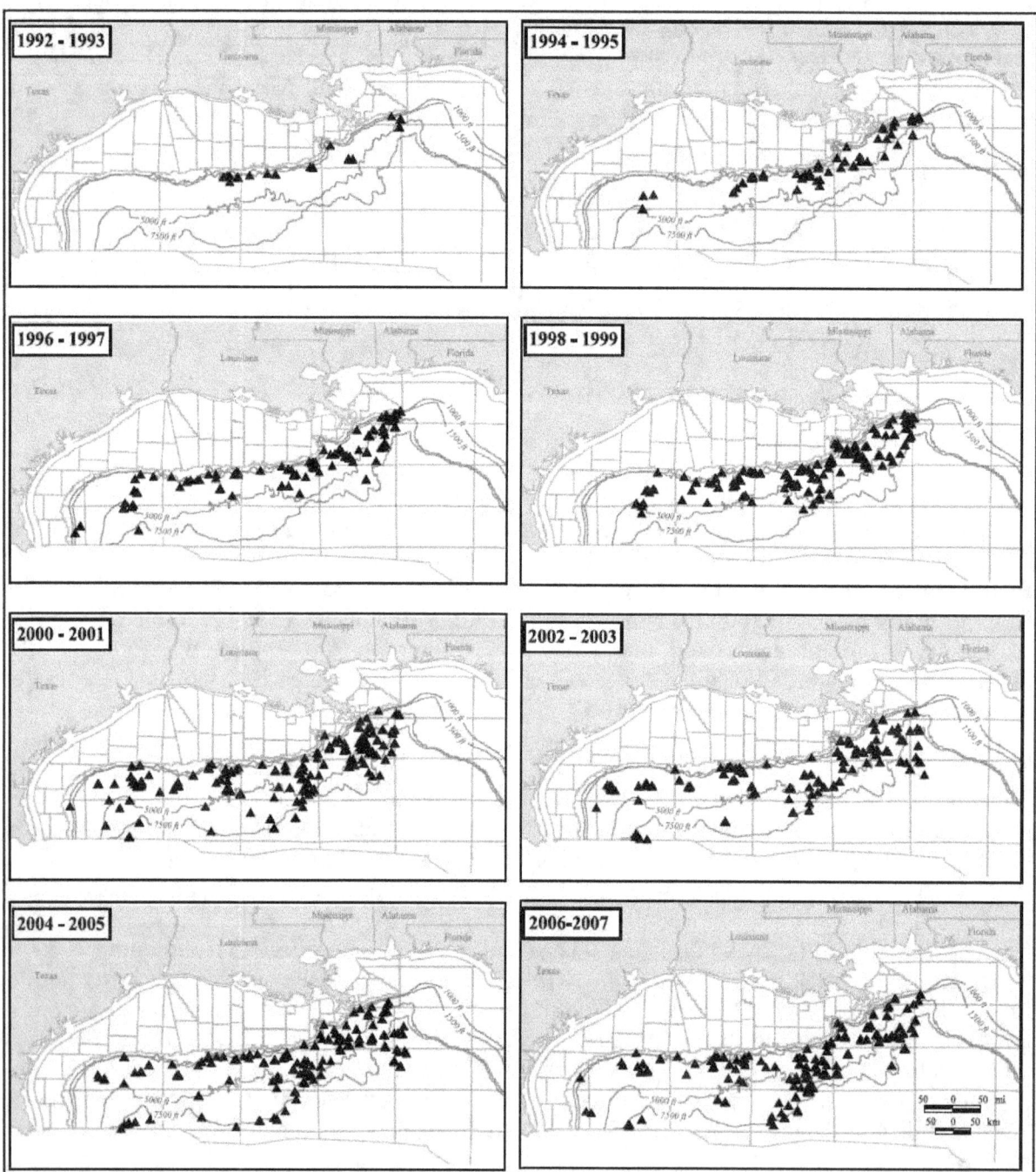

Figure 27. Deepwater exploration wells drilled by years.

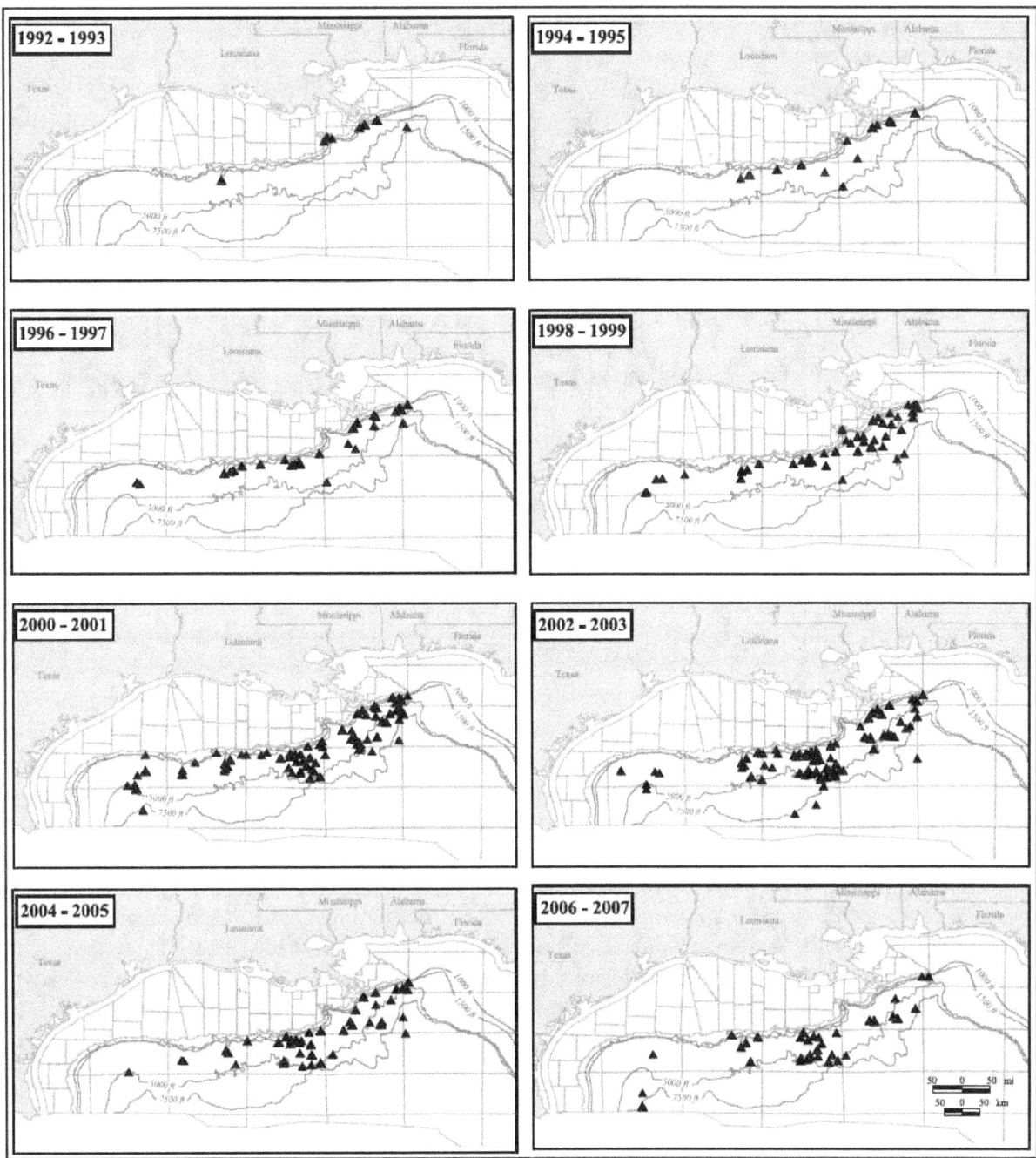

Figure 28. Deepwater development wells drilled by years.

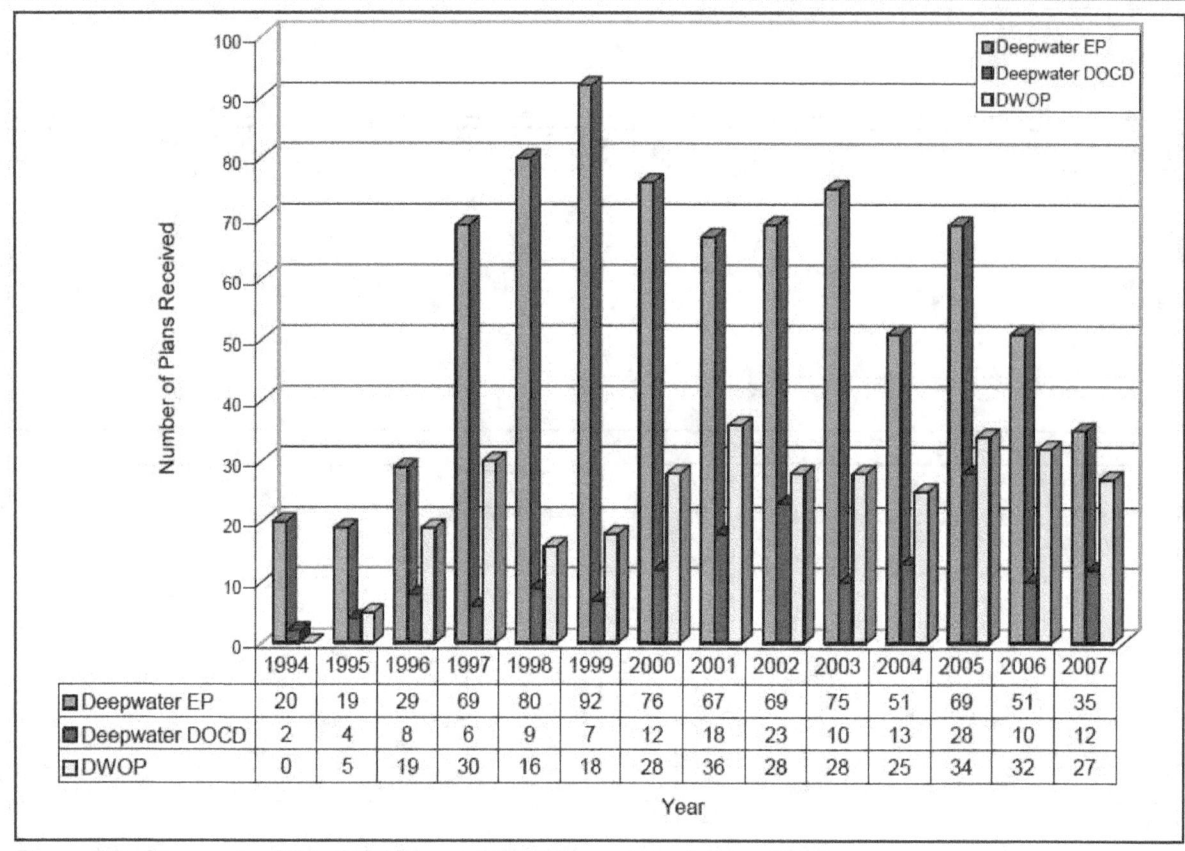

	1994	1995	1996	1997	1998	1999	2000	2001	2002	2003	2004	2005	2006	2007
Deepwater EP	20	19	29	69	80	92	76	67	69	75	51	69	51	35
Deepwater DOCD	2	4	8	6	9	7	12	18	23	10	13	28	10	12
DWOP	0	5	19	30	16	18	28	36	28	28	25	34	32	27

Figure 29. Deepwater EP's, DOCD's, and DWOP's received since 1994.

HIGH PRESSURE, HIGH TEMPERATURE

High-pressure, high-temperature (HP/HT) development is one of the greatest technological and regulatory challenges to the oil and gas industry today. The basic building blocks of structural integrity are being challenged. Metals and elastomers that have been in use for many years now face unique environmental conditions. The MMS is working with industry to evaluate the risks and set limits to mitigate these potential hazards. The MMS is also sponsoring research and participating in internal and industry-related conferences to stay at the forefront of new technology, and MMS is actively involved in developing options that will best promote human safety and environmental integrity. High-pressure, high-temperature compounds the technological challenges faced in deepwater exploration and especially in deepwater completion and production. Consequently, there is tremendous potential for growth and development in the HP/HT area.

NEW TECHNOLOGY

In 2007, new technology applications addressed all areas of deepwater activities, including drilling, completion, production, and workover operations. In addition, MMS personnel and members of the industrial community updated API recommended practices and other regulatory documents to accompany the new technological advances.

Four examples of technology advancements that MMS approved in 2007 include the following: the OmniMAX anchor; the use of pre-set polyester moorings for deepwater drilling rigs; a disconnectable, internal turret mooring system for ship-shape floating production systems; and various forms of subsea boosting, including subsea pump systems that allows enhanced hydrocarbon resource recovery.

OmniMAX Anchor and Mudrope

The OmniMAX anchor (U.S. Patent #7,059,263) is a gravity-installed, vertically-loaded anchor (VLA) with a high modulus polyethylene (HMPE) mudrope forerunner. Unlike other deepwater anchor foundations, the OmniMAX is capable of being loaded in any direction – 360° around the axis of the anchor. Under extreme loading and uplift angle conditions, the anchor will penetrate deeper into the seafloor to gain the needed holding capacity. This anchor technology offers great benefit in the design of mooring systems. It has the potential to reduce the risks to the Gulf's subsea infrastructure in case of station-keeping damage or partial failure of a mooring system. This technology may even allow damaged moorings to survive longer should multiple line failure occur. The anchor's innate ability to receive varying load angle changes without adversely affecting the capacity of its foundation is a significant benefit. The MMS approved the use of the OmniMAX anchor and mudrope system on December 12, 2007. The first OmniMAX anchor installation for offshore oil and gas use in the GOM was completed on December 30, 2007, in Garden Banks Block 667 for use with the *Ocean Star* MODU. This marks the first time a gravity-installed VLA was successfully deployed for offshore OCS use.

Pre-set Polyester Mooring for Deepwater Drilling Rigs

Although the use of polyester mooring lines for station-keeping on production facilities is still considered new technology in the GOM, it is common practice to use this type of technology on MODU's. One stipulation the MMS has required of operators for allowing the use of polyester moorings has traditionally been that the synthetic rope may not come in contact with the seafloor. This requirement limits particle migration into the load-bearing fibers of the rope. In recent years, the oil and gas industry has requested permission to pre-set MODU mooring lines. This procedure results in the rope being laid on the seafloor until the rig is connected to the moorings. Since these lines can be inspected more frequently (generally after each drilling campaign) compared with those of permanently fixed production facilities, MMS was willing to consider these requests. After conducting extensive research on the jacket and filter layer of the synthetic rope, MMS has granted approval for operators to pre-set polyester mooring lines for MODU's with the stipulation that the lines be visually inspected each time they are retrieved. Polyester mooring lines for permanent facilities are still not permitted to touch the seafloor, but MMS has extended the time between scheduled insert removals/testing for these facilities.

Disconnectable Internal Turret System

The turret is the primary interface between a weathervaning, floating production facility and the "stationary" mooring, riser, and subsea systems. The turret acts as the primary load path between these systems. Since the production facility may not be designed to stay on location during a severe storm or hurricane, the turret can be disconnected to allow the facility to sail away from its mooring system. The turret and subsea systems remain on location at a safe depth below the water's surface. The concept of a disconnectable, internal turret system was approved by MMS in the conceptual plan for the Cascade and Chinook Fields. The MMS will require that a bubble-tight, shut-down valve remain with the submerged buoy and a separate bubble-tight, shut-down valve remain with the facility. The MMS will also mandate that the piping located between these valves be able to be flushed before a planned disconnection, thus preventing the release of any liquids to the Gulf's waters.

Subsea Pumping and Separation

Subsea pumping and separation have been identified by the industry as key enablers in improving ultimate recovery from deepwater fields in the GOM. The MMS has approved one application for the King Field, which involved subsea pumping operations. The MMS is currently evaluating two other applications: the Perdido Regional Development hub for subsea pumping and Cascade-Chinook FPSO for a combination of subsea pumping and subsea separation. The pumps will boost the operating system pressure, lowering flowing tubing pressures at each well, thereby increasing flow rates. Shell, BP, and Petrobras are just a few of the many operators using or considering the use of subsea boosting to increase production and extend field life, ultimately increasing hydrocarbon recovery.

Two subsea pumps and associated equipment were installed by BP at the King Field. This installation set a new record for both water depth and tie-back distance. The pumps are located at a water depth of approximately 5,500 ft (1,676 m) and reside more than 15 mi (24 km) from their host, the Marlin tension-leg platform (TLP). The pumps were put into service in December 2007.

DEVELOPMENT SYSTEMS

Development strategies vary for deep water, depending on reserve size, proximity to infrastructure, operating considerations (such as well interventions), economic considerations, and an operator's interest in establishing a production hub for the area. **Appendix A** lists the systems that have begun production, and **Figure 30** shows the location of existing deepwater structures by type in the GOM. Fixed platforms (e.g., Bullwinkle) have economic water-depth limits of about 2,000 ft (610 m). Compliant towers (e.g., Petronius) may be considered for water depths of approximately 1,000 to 2,000 ft (305 to 610 m). Tension-leg platforms (e.g., Brutus, Magnolia, and Marco Polo) are frequently used in 1,000- to 5,000-ft (305- to 1,524-m) water depths. Spars (e.g., Genesis and Red Hawk); semisubmersible production units (e.g., Na Kika); ship-shape, disconnectable floating production units (FPU's); and FPSO systems may be used in water depths ranging up to and beyond 10,000 ft (3,048 m). **Figure 31** is a graphic representation of the various types of production systems.

Fixed Platform

A fixed platform consists of a welded tubular steel jacket, deck, and surface facility. The jacket and deck make up the foundation for the surface facilities. The jacket is secured by piles driven into the seafloor. The height of the platform is dictated by the water depth at the intended location. Once the jacket is secured and a deck is installed, additional

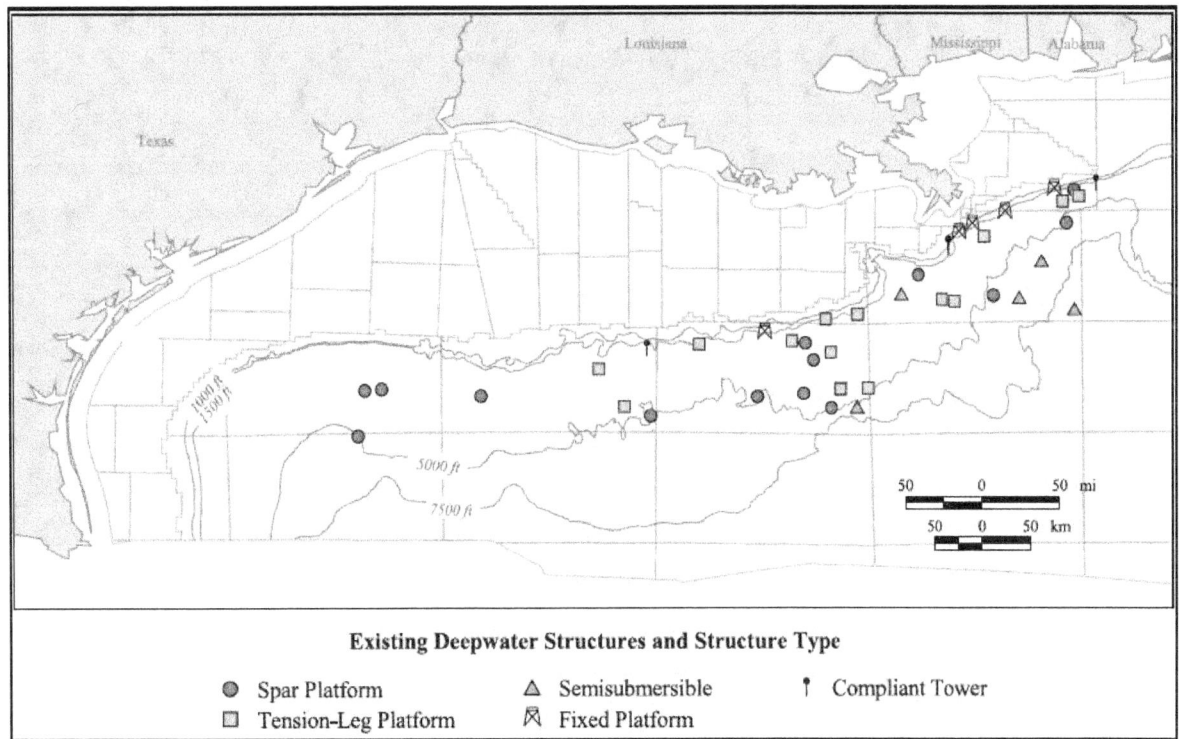

Existing Deepwater Structures and Structure Type

● Spar Platform   △ Semisubmersible   ⸸ Compliant Tower

□ Tension-Leg Platform   ⊠ Fixed Platform

Figure 30. Location map of currently installed deepwater structures by type.

modules are added for drilling, production, and crew operations. Large barge-mounted cranes are used in positioning and securing the jacket and the installation of the topside modules. Economic considerations hinder development of fixed (rigid) platforms in water depths greater than 2,000 ft (610 m).

Compliant Tower

A compliant tower consists of a narrow tower and a piled foundation. Unlike a fixed platform, a compliant tower has greater flexibility and can withstand large lateral forces by sustaining significant lateral deflections. It is usually deployed in water depths between 1,000 and 2,000 ft (305 and 610 m).

Tension-Leg Platform

A tension-leg platform (TLP) is a compliant structural system vertically moored and uses buoyant components to maintain tension in the mooring system. ConocoPhillips successfully installed the deepest TLP in the world at Magnolia (Garden Banks Block 783) in December 2004 in 4,674 ft (1,425 m) of water.

Semisubmersible Production Unit

A semisubmersible production platform is a floating system that may have drilling capabilities. It comprises the following major components: pontoons, columns, and a large deck. The pontoons and columns provide buoyancy to the system. Production equipment,

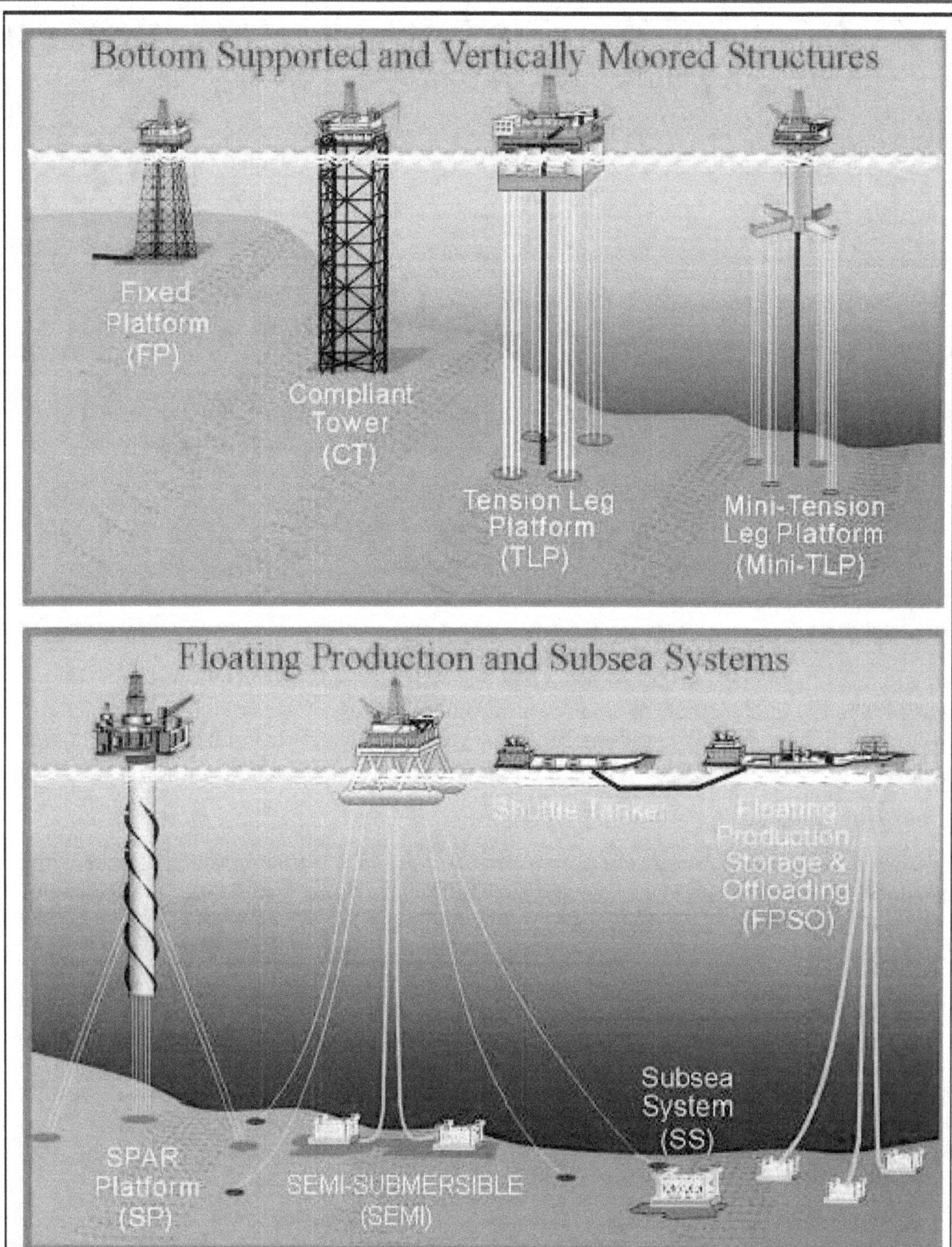

Figure 31. Deepwater development systems.

living quarters, and storage space are assembled on the deck. Semisubmersibles are permanently moored, using various anchoring techniques, and can be operated in a wide range of water depths.

Independence Hub, the world's deepest semisubmersible production unit, was installed in approximately 8,000 ft (2,438 m) of water. Located in Mississippi Canyon Block 920, this facility has the capacity to produce 1 Bcf/d from up to 27 flowlines. Currently, 15 wells are on production in 10 different subsea fields. The water depths of the wells range from 7,787 ft (2,373 m) at San Jacinto to 8,960 ft (2,731 m) at Cheyenne.

Another deepwater semisubmersible to gain world wide interest is the Thunder Horse Facility. As the world's largest semisubmersible production unit, the 59,500-ton Thunder Horse production, drilling, and quarters (PDQ) unit, arrived in the GOM in 2004 from Korea. The topside modules, fabricated in Morgan City, Louisiana, were installed in Ingleside, Texas. The Thunder Horse unit was nearly 4 years in the making and will develop the largest discovery ever made in the GOM. When fully operational, the unit will be capable of producing an astounding 250 Mbo/d and 200 MMcf/d. The installation of Thunder Horse (Mississippi Canyon Block 778) was delayed by Hurricane Dennis in 2005 and by metallurgy issues in 2006 and 2007. Thunder Horse is expected to begin limited production in 2008 with additional wells going on production in 2009.

Floating Production Unit (FPU) and Floating Production, Storage, and Offloading (FPSO) Facility

An FPU is traditionally a ship-shape vessel capable of processing production from subsea facilities, but without storage capability. Some gas is used to fuel the vessel, and the excess gas, along with all the oil, is transported to market via export pipelines. Similarly, an FPSO is traditionally a ship-shape vessel capable of processing production from subsea facilities, but it has the capacity to store produced fluids and offload via a shuttle vessel at a later date. Gas is used to fuel the FPSO with the excess being exported via an export pipeline.

An FPU and FPSO may be moored via conventional mooring lines, synthetic mooring lines, or may be dynamically positioned. Mooring lines and risers are connected to the vessel via a disconnectable turret/buoy system (DTS) for all the currently proposed GOM facilities. This allows the ship to sail to a safer location during an extreme weather event. The DTS, including the mooring lines and risers, remain submerged at a pre-determined depth after disconnection. This minimizes the impact of extreme weather situations and does not impede marine transportation.

The GOM's first application for the use of an FPSO was submitted in May 2007. Petrobras America Inc. plans to develop the Cascade and Chinook Fields located in Walker Ridge with a moored, disconnectable FPSO. Production from the fields' subsea wells is transported via flowlines to the free-standing hybrid risers (FSHR), another first for the Gulf. These risers are connected to the FPSO through the DTS. Gas will depart the FPSO via an export FSHR to the export pipeline. Oil will be stored on the facility until it is periodically offloaded to a shuttle vessel for transshipment to onshore receiving terminals. First oil from both fields is expected in 2010 with further expansion possible in the future.

In anticipation of this application, MMS and the U.S. Coast Guard (USCG) developed a new Memorandum of Agreement (MOA) for floating production facilities. This agreement lays the groundwork for determining each agencies regulatory responsibility.

Another first for the GOM was Energy Resource Technology, Inc.'s application for a ship-shape, dynamically positioned (DP), disconnectable turret FPU for the Phoenix development. The disconnectable turret system on this facility is not designed as a structural mooring component because of the DP capability. Since there is no storage capability on the FPU, oil and gas will be transported via export risers to pipelines.

Spar

A spar is a vessel with a circular cross-section that sits vertically in the water and is supported by buoyancy chambers (hard tanks) at the top, a flooded mid-section structure hanging from the hard tanks, and a stabilizing keel section at the bottom. A spar is held in place by a catenary mooring system, providing lateral stability. Currently, there are three competing versions of spars used in the GOM: classic spar, truss spar, and cell spar.

Shell Offshore Inc. recently announced that they will be installing the deepest spar production facility in Alaminos Canyon. The Perdido Regional Development hub will be located in about 8,000 ft (2,438 m) water depth to develop the Great White, Tobago, and Silvertip Fields. Once operating at full capacity, Perdido will be capable of handling 130,000 BOE/d.

Subsea Systems

Subsea systems are capable of producing hydrocarbons from reservoirs covering the entire range of water depths that industry is exploring. Subsea systems continue to be a key component in the success in deep water to date. In fact, 85 percent of all currently producing deepwater fields utilize subsea systems (**Figure 32**). These systems are generally multi-component seafloor facilities that allow the production of hydrocarbons in water depths that would normally preclude installing conventional fixed or bottom-founded platforms. The subsea system can be divided into two major components: the seafloor equipment and the surface equipment. The seafloor equipment will include some or all of the following: one or more subsea wells, manifolds, control umbilicals, pumping or processing equipment, and flowlines. The surface component of the subsea system includes the control system and other production equipment located on a host platform that could be located many miles from the actual wells. The economics of deepwater development have improved by connecting multiple subsea projects to a single hub. For example, the Independence Hub facility supports 10 separate producing fields.

SUBSEA TRENDS

Figure 33 shows the number of subsea completions each year since 1988 (only productive wells were counted). There were fewer than 10 subsea completions per year until 1993. In 2001 and 2002, dramatic increases in deepwater subsea completions occurred. These increases are partially attributable to fields associated with the Na Kika floating production facility. At this same time, subsea completions in deep water dramatically overshadowed those in shallow water. In 2007, a record was set for the highest number of subsea completions in deep water, many of which were associated with the Independence Hub facility. The pie chart in **Figure 33** shows that deepwater subsea wells constitute the majority (63%) of the total subsea well population in the GOM.

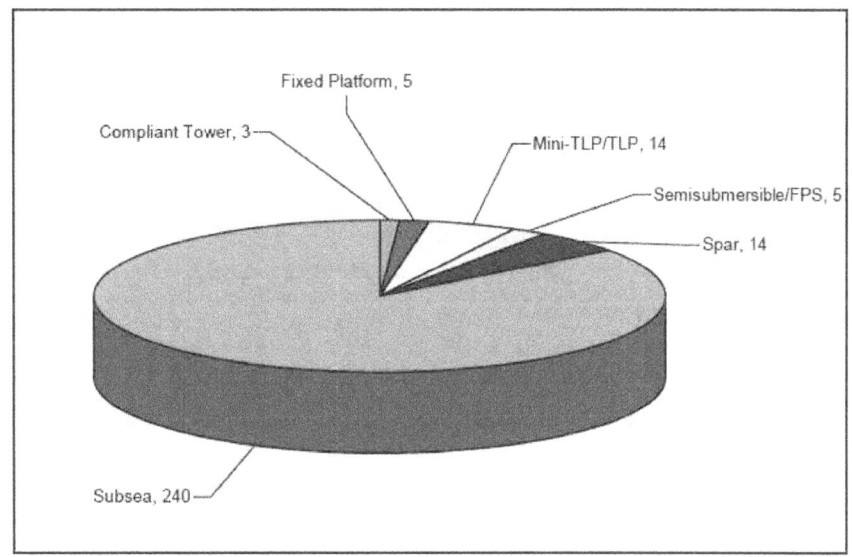

Figure 32. Production systems for currently producing fields, including subsea systems.

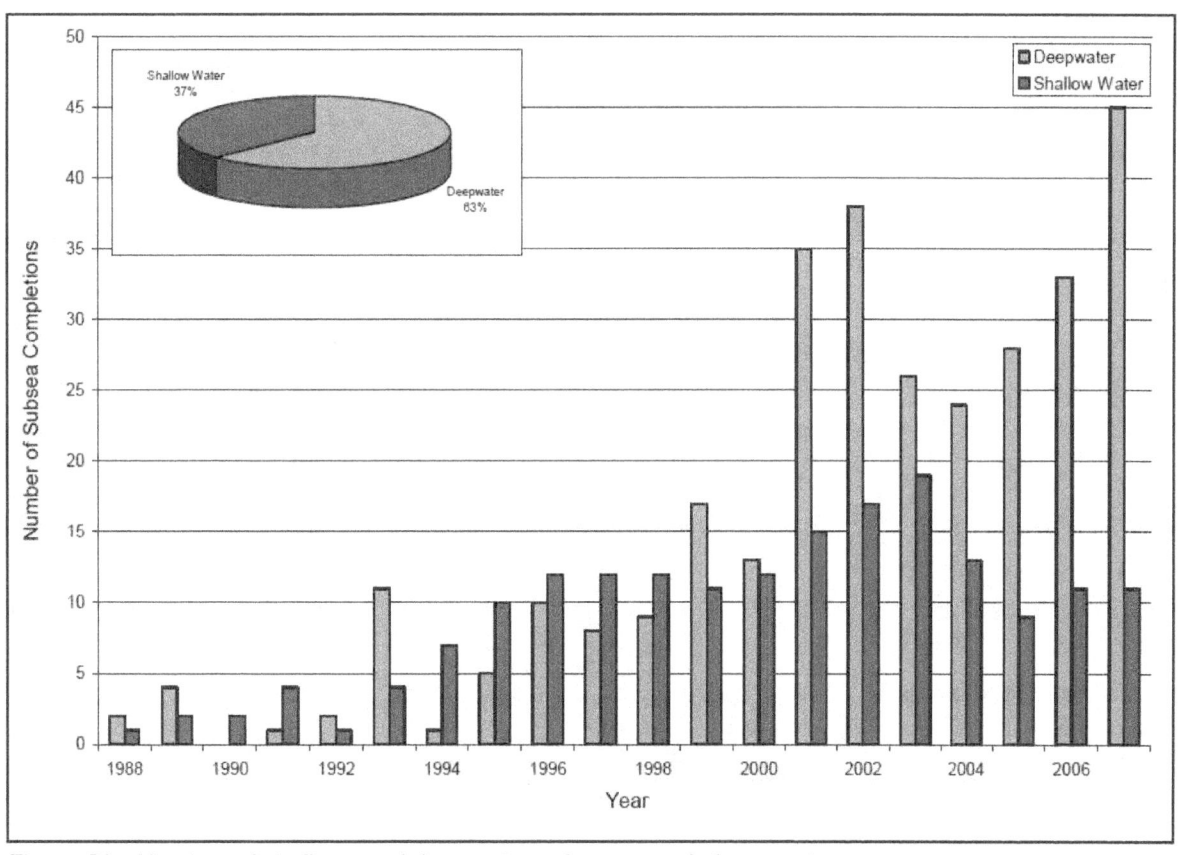

Figure 33. Number of shallow- and deepwater subsea completions each year.

The technology required to implement subsea production systems in deep water have evolved significantly. This evolution is apparent in **Figure 34**, which shows that the deepest subsea completion was in 350 ft (107 m) of water until 1988, when the water depth record jumped to 2,243 ft or 684 m (Green Canyon Block 31 project). In 1996, another record was reached with a subsea completion in 2,956 ft (901 m) of water (Mars project), followed by a 1997 subsea completion in 5,295 ft (1,614 m) of water (Mensa project). Cheyenne, one of the subsea fields tying back to the Independence Hub facility, has the deepest subsea completion in the GOM to date, in a water depth of 8,960 ft (2,731 m). Last year, a subsea well was completed at a water depth of 8,807 ft (2,684 m) in the Atlas NW Field, which is also tied back to Independence Hub. A listing of productive subsea and temporarily abandoned completions in the GOM can be found in **Appendix C**.

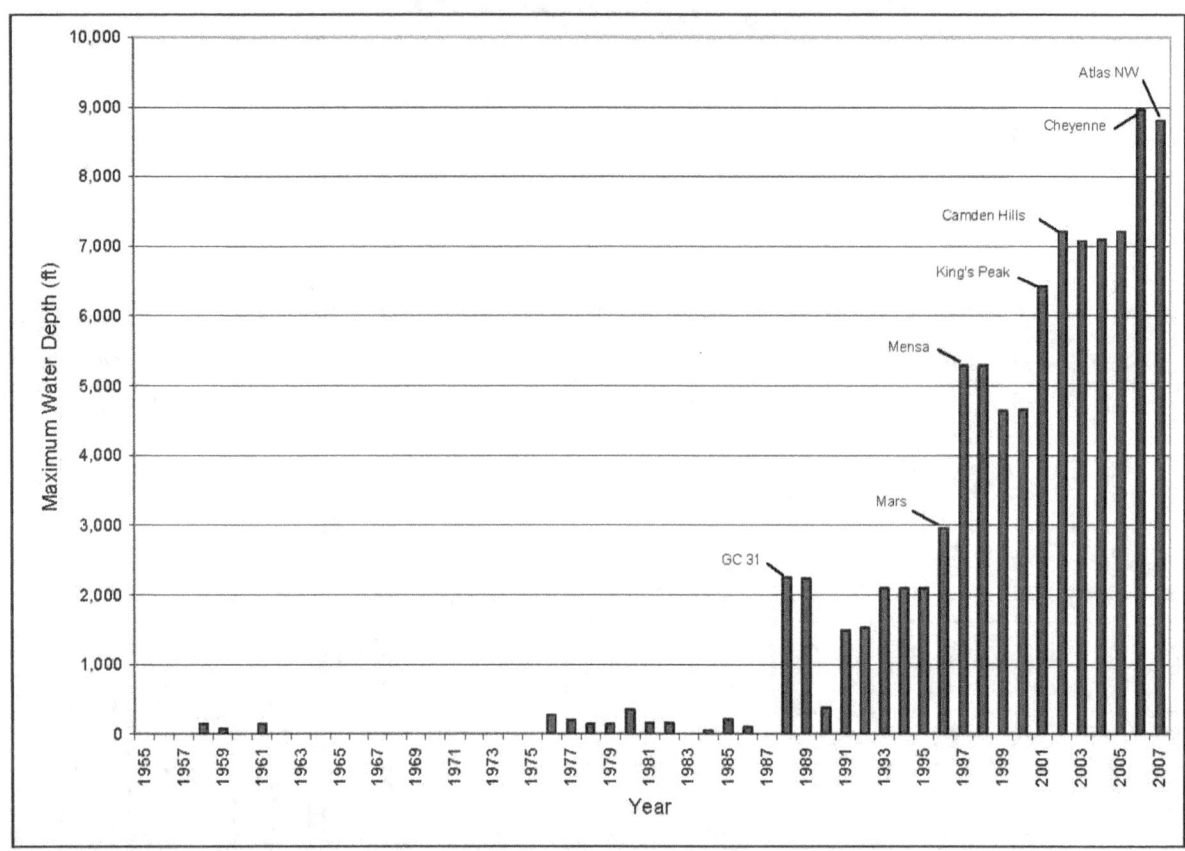

Figure 34. Maximum water depth of subsea completions installed each year.

NEW DEVELOPMENTS

Deepwater development is constantly evolving and expanding in the GOM. As new discoveries are made, operators must determine the most efficient and economical means of recovering those hydrocarbon reserves. Where possible, an operator may decide to use subsea technology to control and produce its deepwater wells within a field. The wells will be tied back to existing infrastructure through flowlines. Other times, either because of operational conditions, logistics, or the magnitude of the discovery, operators may decide to install a production facility. While there are over 50 deepwater production facilities currently installed, there are many more in the planning and development phases.

Independence Hub – Anadarko Petroleum Corporation

The world-record-setting Independence Hub project began producing natural gas from the ultra-deep waters of the GOM in July 2007. Operated by Anadarko Petroleum Corporation and owned by Enterprise (80%) and Helix (20%), Independence Hub is the Gulf's largest and deepest natural gas processing facility with capacity to bring 1 Bcf/d of natural gas to American consumers. The layout of the project spans a massive 142 blocks or about 1,800 mi^2 (over 4,600 km^2) in waters of up to 9,000 ft (2,745 m) deep and will account for over 10 percent of all natural gas currently produced from the GOM. At year-end 2007, Independence Hub was producing more than 900 MMcf/d from 10 discoveries – 8 of which are operated by Anadarko.

Atlantis – BP America Inc

On December 18, 2007, BP announced that it had completed commissioning of the Atlantis semisubmersible platform in the deepwater GOM and commenced the export of oil and gas from the deepest moored, floating oil and gas production facility in the world. Gas sales have started and oil volumes are increasing as the facility ramps up production. Additional wells will continue to be brought on stream, and the facility is expected to reach plateau production by the end of 2008. The Atlantis semisubmersible platform is designed to process 200,000 barrels of oil and 180 million cubic feet of gas per day.

Shenzi – BHP Billiton

In 2006, BHP Billiton sanctioned the development of the Shenzi Field, located in the deep waters of the CPA. An early phase of production commenced in October 2007 from the western portion of the field, which was previously known as Genghis Khan and acquired from the initial leaseholder (Anadarko) earlier in the year. Production from the Genghis Khan portion of the field will be transported to the Marco Polo TLP in Green Canyon Block 608. This TLP is a third-party facility operated by Anadarko. Development of the eastern portion of the field (Shenzi) is on schedule to commence production in mid-2009. The Shenzi production facility will feature a TLP with a design capacity for 100,000 bo/d and 50 MMcf/d of natural gas. Together, these projects comprise a six-block development area in Green Canyon (Blocks 608, 609, 610, 652, 653, and 654) for which BHP Billiton serves as operator, with 44 percent. Other partners in the conjoined projects are Hess and Repsol YPF with 28 percent each.

Thunder Horse – BP America Inc.

The Thunder Horse project is currently preparing for start up of production in 2008 and is one of the key discoveries upon which BP will grow its future deepwater development in the GOM. Designed to process 250,000 bo/d and 200 MMcf/d of natural gas, Thunder Horse will be the largest producer in the Gulf. The field lies approximately 150 mi (241 km) southeast of New Orleans in about 6,000 ft (1,829 m) of water. High-pressure, high-temperature reservoirs in multiple intervals are distributed from 18,000 to 24,000 ft (5,486 to 7,315 m) subsea. All of the 21 pipeline end terminations (plets) and the temporary manifolds have now been installed. Change-out of the first tree (Mississippi Canyon Block 822 well #3) at drill center 45 by the Enterprise MODU was completed in December 2007. The remaining scope of work before first production from the South field includes the installation of jumpers and the commissioning of the production system.

Perdido – Shell Exploration and Production Company

The Perdido Regional Development host facility will be located in Alaminos Canyon Block 857. Once installed, the direct vertical access truss spar will set a new record as the deepest spar in over 8,000 ft (2,438 m) of water depth. The Perdido spar will be capable of handling 130,000 BOE/d (100,000 bo/d and 200 MMcf/d) from the wells located directly below the structure (part of the Great White Field) as well as subsea tiebacks from other portions of the Great White Field and the Silvertip and Tobago Fields. As a part of the Perdido development concept, Shell has requested approval for a subsea separation/boosting system to enhance overall recovery from the fields. Perdido is expected to come on production in 2010.

Cascade-Chinook – Petrobras America Inc.

In 2007, Petrobras America Inc. (Petrobras) submitted a DWOP and DOCD to develop the Cascade-Chinook Fields with the Gulf's first FPSO. The Cascade Field (Walker Ridge Block 206 Unit – Blocks 205, 206, 249, and 250) is located approximately 250 mi (402 km) south of New Orleans and about 165 mi (266 km) from the Louisiana coastline in approximately 8,200 ft (2,499 m) of water. The Chinook Field (Walker Ridge Block 425 Unit – Blocks 425, 426, 469, and 470) is located about 16 mi (26 km) south of the Cascade Prospect in approximately 8,800 ft (2,682 m) of water. The FPSO will be located in the southeast corner of Walker Ridge Block 249 in a water depth of about 8,200 ft (2,499 m). The FPSO will be a converted, double-hulled, ship-shape vessel owned by BW Offshore with a storage capacity of approximately 600,000 barrels, a process capacity of 80,000 bo/d, and gas export facilities of 16 MMscf/d.

Petrobras has proposed the use of five new technologies in the development of their fields: FPSO with a disconnectable turret; crude oil transportation via shuttle vessels [i.e., shuttle tanker, integrated tug barge (ITB), or articulated tug barge (ATB)]; subsea electric submersible pump (ESP); FSHR; and a polyester mooring system.

In the initial development phase, Petrobras proposes to drill and complete two new wells in the Cascade Field and a single new well in the Chinook Field. The subsea production wells would be tied back to the FPSO using dual 9 5/8-in (24.4-cm) flowlines and FSHR's. Production will be enhanced by subsea booster pumps that are located downstream from the gathering manifolds. The FPSO will separate and treat the production and store the liquid hydrocarbon within the vessel. **Figure 35** is an artistic rendering that depicts the proposed two-field development infrastructure and displays the FPSO and shuttle vessel in a tandem configuration. Subsequent development phases for the project may include up to 24 additional wells. First oil is expected in 2010.

Produced crude oil will be transported by shuttle vessels from the FPSO to a port along the U.S. Gulf Coast. Produced gas will be used to fuel the common process facilities on the FPSO. Excess gas will be transported from the FPSO via a FSHR and a 6-in (25-cm) export pipeline that will connect to the existing GOM pipeline infrastructure.

Petrobras is currently considering two tie-in options for their development: the "Cleopatra Option" (operated by BP) is located in Green Canyon Block 829 and is approximately 43 mi (69 km) from the FPSO, and the "Anaconda Option" (operated by Enterprise) is located in Green Canyon Block 606 and is approximately 66 mi (106 km) from the FPSO.

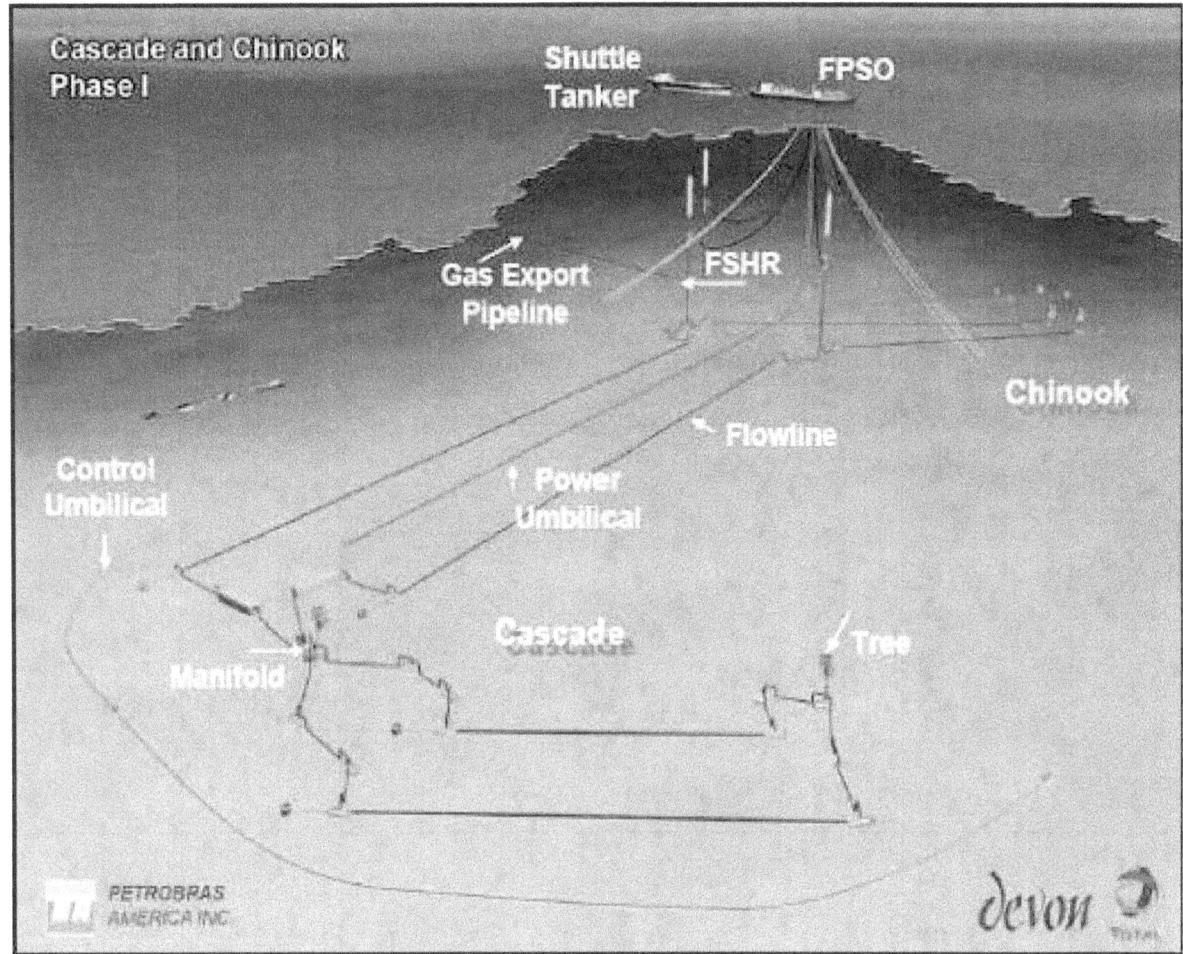

Figure 35. Infrastructure schematic of the Cascade and Chinook Field development, Phase I (image courtesy of Petrobras and Devon).

NEW PIPELINES

The pipeline infrastructure to bring deepwater oil and gas onshore also expanded during the 1990's. The pipeline from a subsea completion to the host platform is commonly referred to as the tieback. The tieback length varies considerably, as shown in **Figure 36**. Most subsea wells are within 10 mi (16 km) of the host platform, with the Mensa Field remaining the current world record holder for a subsea tieback length of 62 mi (100 km) from the host platform. The second longest subsea tieback in the world (55 mi or 88 km) is Canyon Express, linking the Aconcagua, Camden Hills, and King's Peak projects to their host platform. The Independence Hub is a prime example of the emerging dependence on subsea tiebacks. The hub uses 192.7 mi (310 km) of flowlines, with the longest tieback stretching over 45 mi (72 km).

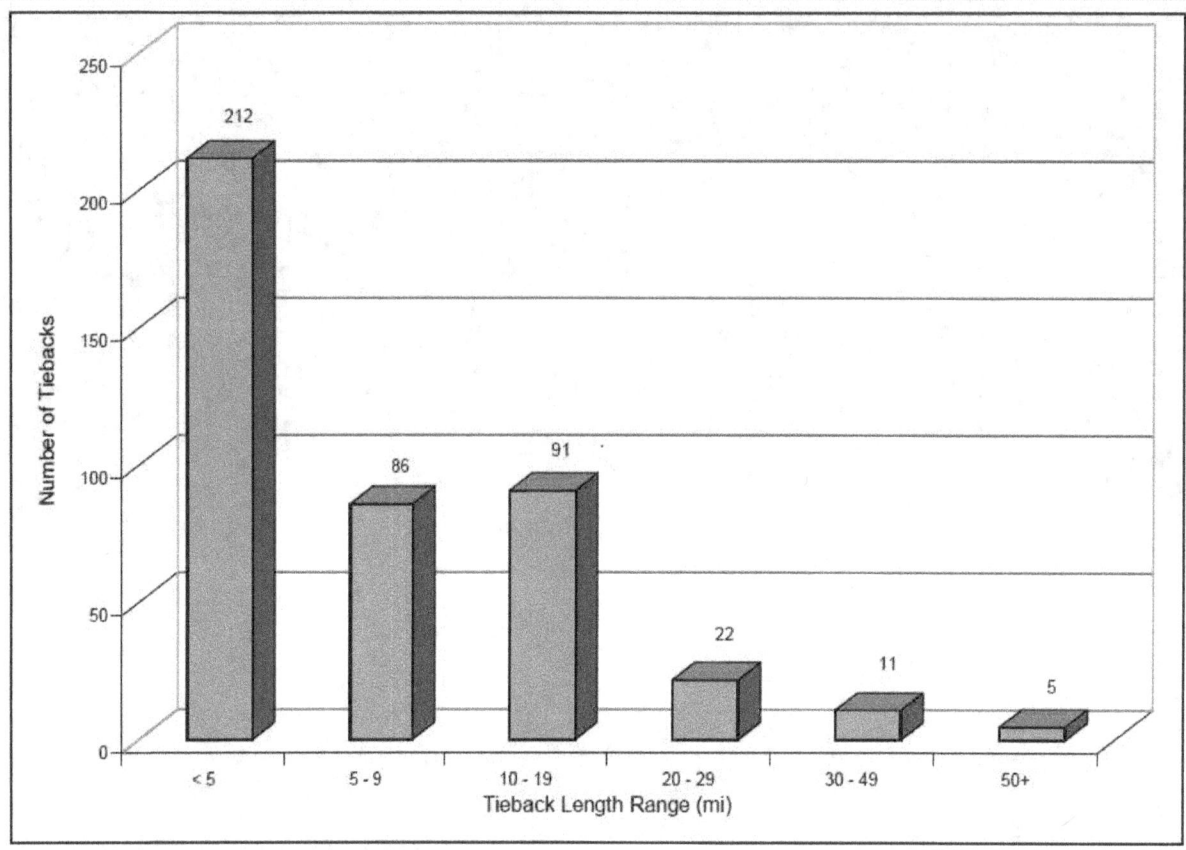

Figure 36. Length of subsea tiebacks.

Deepwater pipelines approved for installation are shown in **Figures 37a** and **37b**. The data include the total length of all pipelines originating at a deepwater development, including any shallow-water segments (control umbilicals are excluded). **Figure 37a** shows deepwater pipelines that are less than or equal to 12 in (30.5 cm) in diameter. Gas pipelines in deep water account for 61 percent of the total approved miles since 1995. The large increase in 2001 in oil and gas pipeline miles reflects approvals for Canyon Express (Aconcagua, Camden Hills, and King's Peak Fields), Horn Mountain, and the Boomvang-Nansen projects. In 2002, projects associated with the Na Kika floating production facility contribute significantly to the mileage. Part of the peak in 2005 is associated with pipelines approved for the Independence Hub, Gomez, and Triton projects. Shenzi, Atlantis, Independence Hub, and Tahiti contributed to last year's totals.

Approval of large pipelines [greater than 12 in (30.5 cm) in diameter] peaked in 1999, primarily from the pipelines associated with Hoover (**Figure 37b**). A dramatic increase occurred in 2002 after a brief downturn in activity in 2000 and 2001. The peak in 2002 was driven by the approval of the Mardi Gras system. Gas and oil from the Mardi Gras system is delivered to onshore processing facilities via the new Cameron Highway pipeline system, which has been a very important development in pipeline infrastructure. Both the Gunnison and Genghis Khan projects contributed to the 2003 totals, while approvals for pipelines associated with Constitution contributed to the totals in 2005. In 2007, the major contributor to the oil pipeline mileage was Shenzi, while Poseidon and Triton bolstered the gas pipeline mileage.

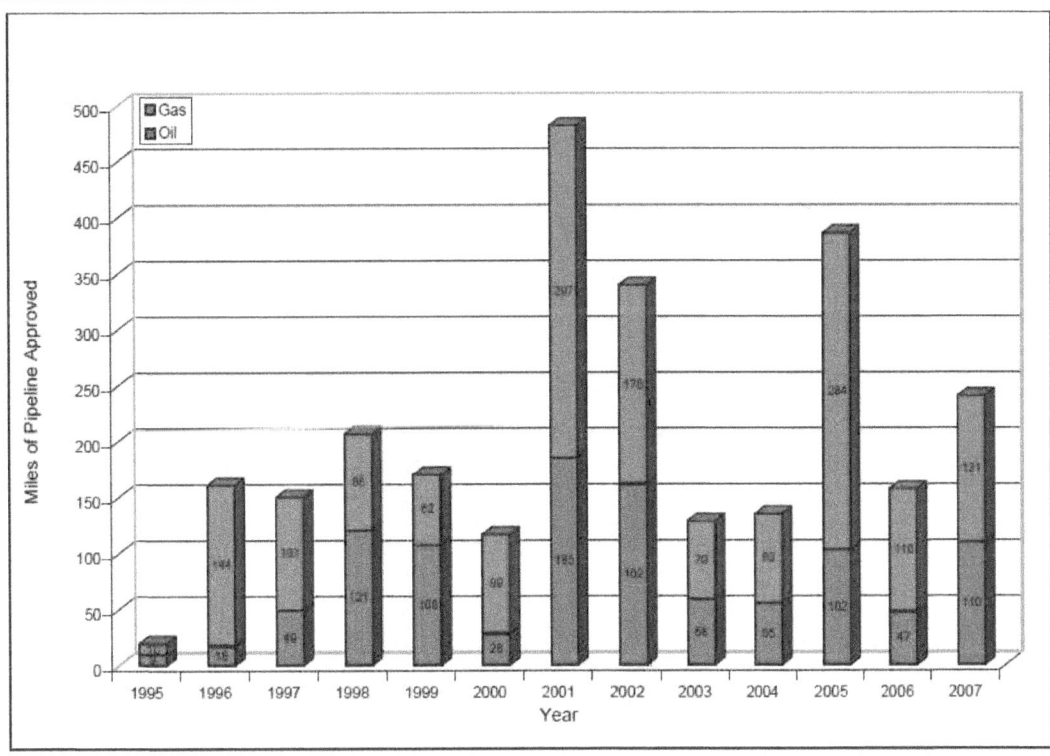

Figure 37a. Approved deepwater oil and gas pipelines less than or equal to 12 inches in diameter.

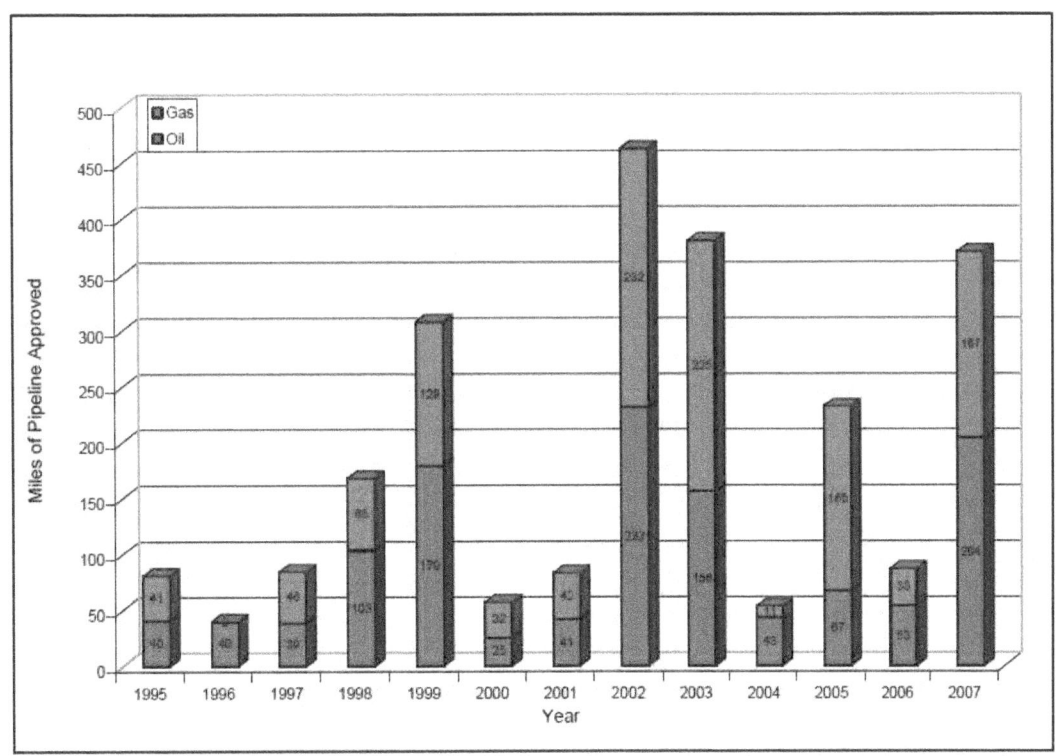

Figure 37b. Approved deepwater oil and gas pipelines greater than 12 inches in diameter.

The infrastructure needed to bring deepwater production online continues to develop over time. **Figure 38** shows the framework of major oil and gas pipelines in the entire GOM. **Figure 39** illustrates the existing oil and gas network of pipelines in deep water. These figures include new and proposed pipelines through the end of 2007.

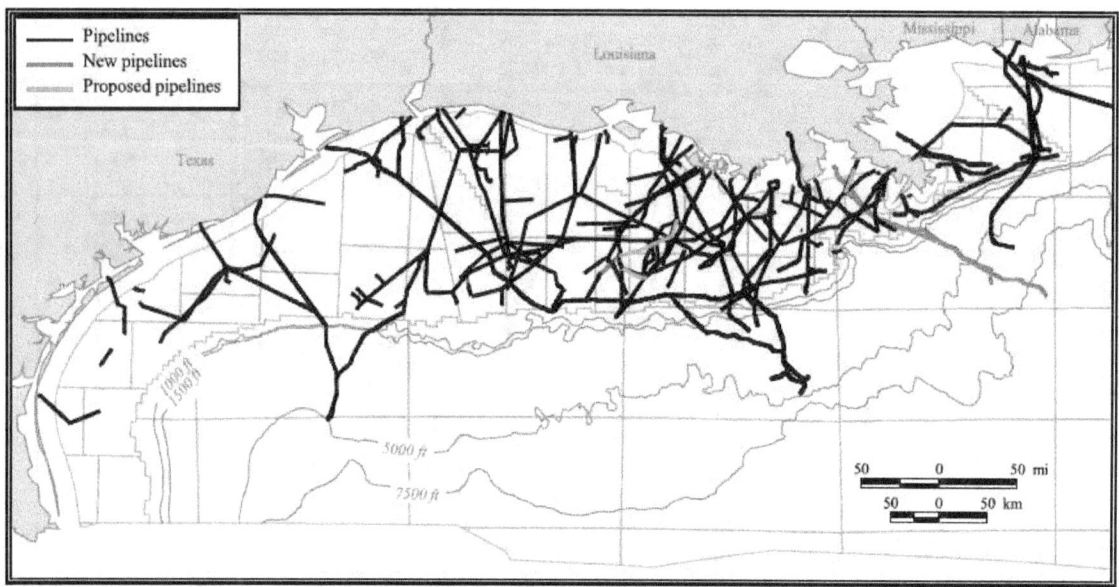

Figure 38. Oil and gas pipelines with diameters greater than or equal to 20 inches.

HIGH-INTEGRITY PRESSURE PROTECTION SYSTEM (HIPPS)

The longer subsea tiebacks being used to develop marginal deepwater fields pose another challenge for industry, namely in the design and installation of pipelines rated for the HP/HT well's shut-in tubing pressure (SITP) of greater than or equal to 15,000 pounds per square inch (psi) and/or 350° F (177° C). Rather than relying on the physical strength of steel to withstand the SITP, a high-integrity pressure protection system (HIPPS) provides alternate over-pressure protection for a pipeline or flowline. The HIPPS employs valves, logic controllers, and pressure transmitters to shut down the system before a pipeline is overpressured and/or ruptured.

The MMS has been working with API to formulate the regulatory framework for the installation of a HIPPS in the GOM. The API resumed work on its *Recommended Practice API RP 17 O, High Integrity Pressure Protection Systems (HIPPS)*, in 2007 (API, in preparation). The MMS is actively working with industry to complete this document by the end of 2008. To date, MMS has approved the concept of a HIPPS, but a formal application has not yet been received.

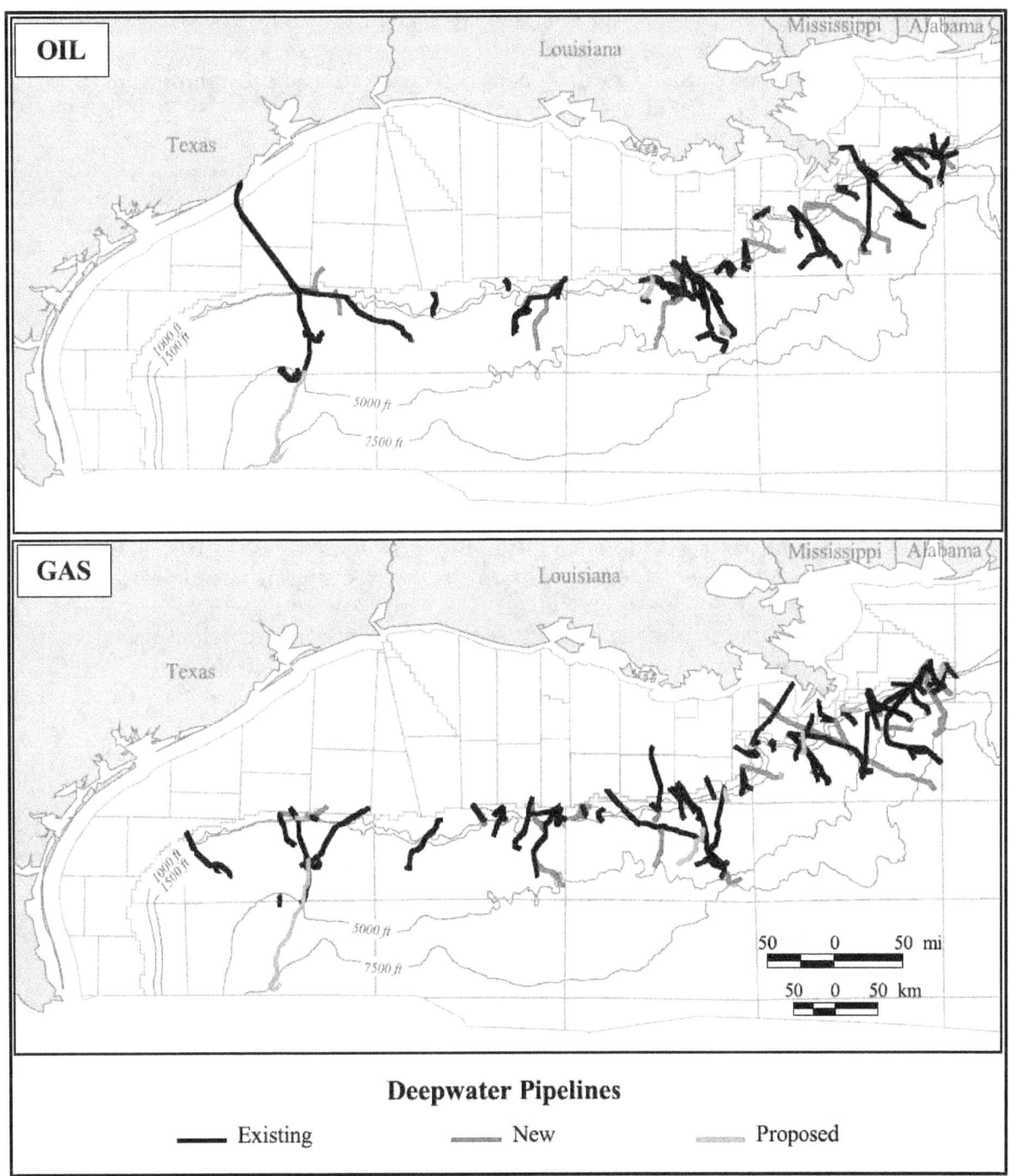

Figure 39. Deepwater oil and gas pipelines.

RESERVES AND PRODUCTION

The deepwater GOM has contributed major additions to the total reserves in the GOM. **Figure 40** shows the proved reserves added each year by water-depth category. Additions from the shallow waters of the GOM declined in recent years but, beginning in 1975, the deepwater area started contributing significant new reserves. Between 1975 and 1983, the majority of these additions were from discoveries in slightly more than 1,000 ft (305 m) of water. It was not until 1985 that major additions came from water depths greater than 1,500 ft (457 m). From 1998 to 2001, significant proved reserves were added in the 5,000- to 7,499-ft (1,524- to 2,286-m) water depth range. The year 2002 saw the first substantial addition from water depths greater than 7,500 ft (2,286 m).

There is often a significant lag between a successful exploration well and its hydrocarbons being produced. The success of an exploration well may remain concealed from the public for several years until the operator requests a "Determination of Well Producibility" from MMS. A successful MMS determination then "qualifies" the lease as producible and the discovery is placed in a field. The discovery date of that field is then defined as the total depth (TD) date of the field's first well that encountered significant hydrocarbons. Hydrocarbon reserves are still considered unproved until it is clear that the field will go on production. Then the reserves move into MMS's proved category. **Figure 41** includes both proved and unproved reserves for each water-depth category. This figure shows declining reserve additions in shallow water, similar to **Figure 40**, but reveals significantly more deepwater reserve additions and large significant unproved reserve additions in water depths greater than 5,000 ft (1,524 m) beginning in 1998.

Figure 42 illustrates the most important feature of the deepwater field discoveries, that their average size is many times larger than the average size of shallow-water fields. Generally over the past 10 years, the field sizes in ultra-deep water are many times larger than shallower-water fields.

It is important to note that MMS has not completed all of the estimates of proved and unproved reserves for 2006 and 2007 discoveries in deep water, thus the proved and unproved reserves additions and average field size for these years are subject to change in future reports. Additionally, some new discoveries on leases for 2006 and 2007 may be placed in existing older fields, resulting in changes to proved and unproved reserves additions and average field size for previous years.

DISCOVERIES

Figure 43 shows the number of deepwater fields discovered each year (according to MMS criteria) and the number of those that began production through 2006. The number of field discoveries for any given year is usually greater than the number of fields that actually go on production. The difference between the number of field discoveries and the number of those that actually produce increased in the early 2000's, because these recent field discoveries have not had ample time for project approval and design and subsequent production. Because of this lag between exploratory drilling and project approval, the full impact of recent, large deepwater exploratory successes is not yet reflected in MMS's proved reserve estimates.

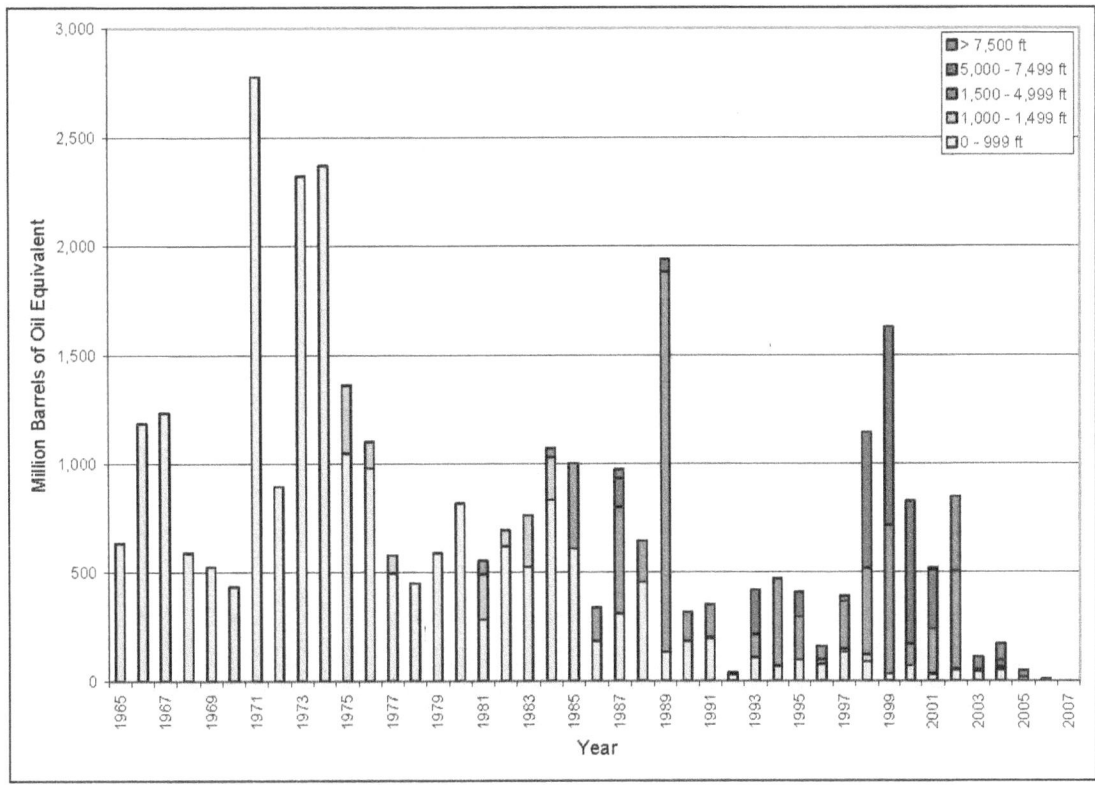

Figure 40. Proved reserve additions.

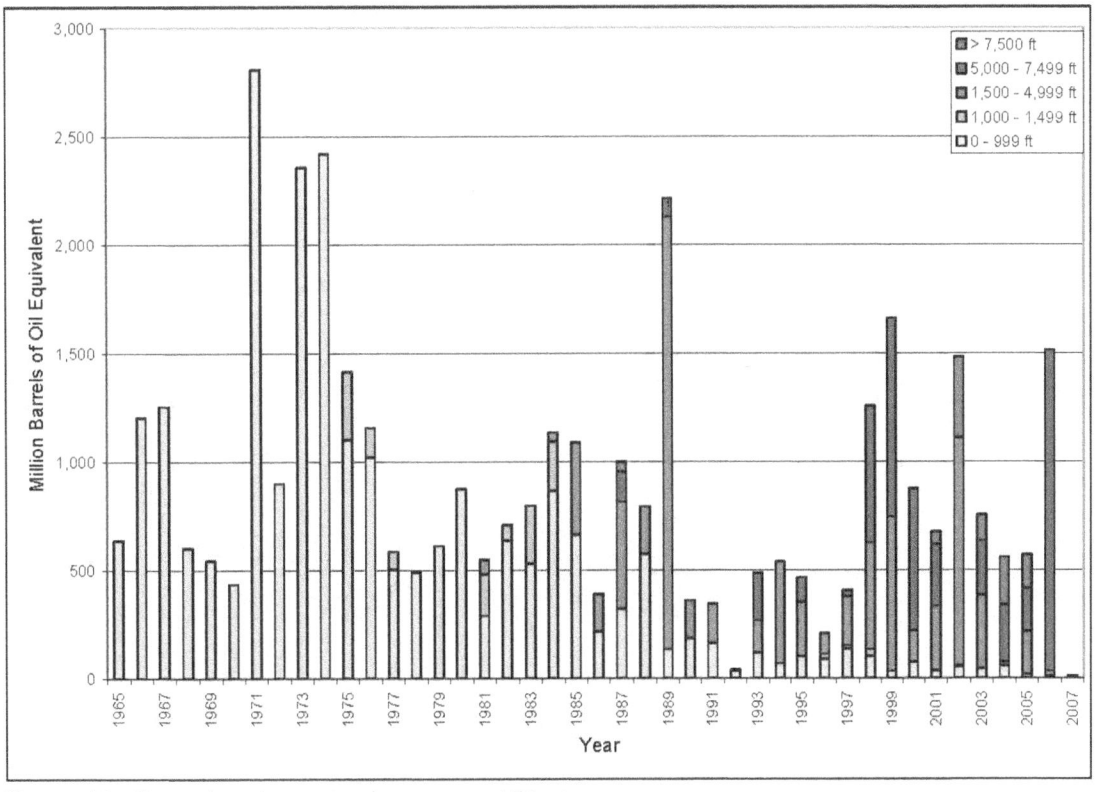

Figure 41. Proved and unproved reserve additions.

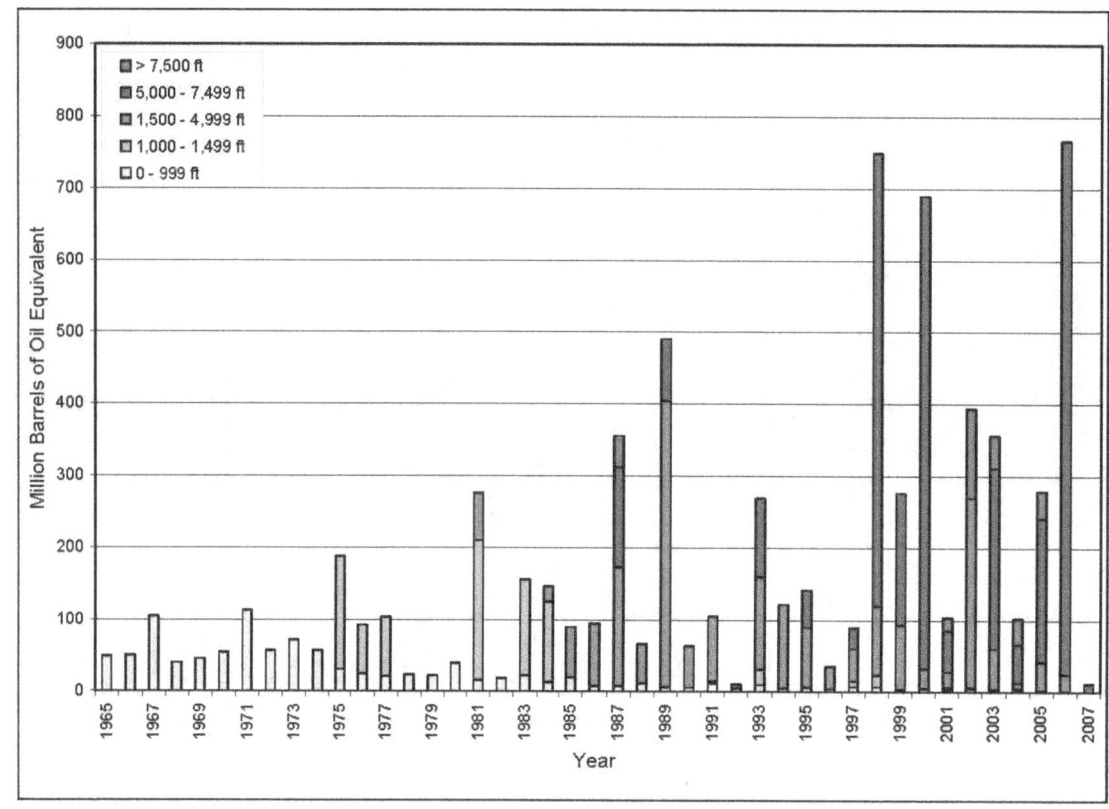

Figure 42. Average field size using proved and unproved reserves.

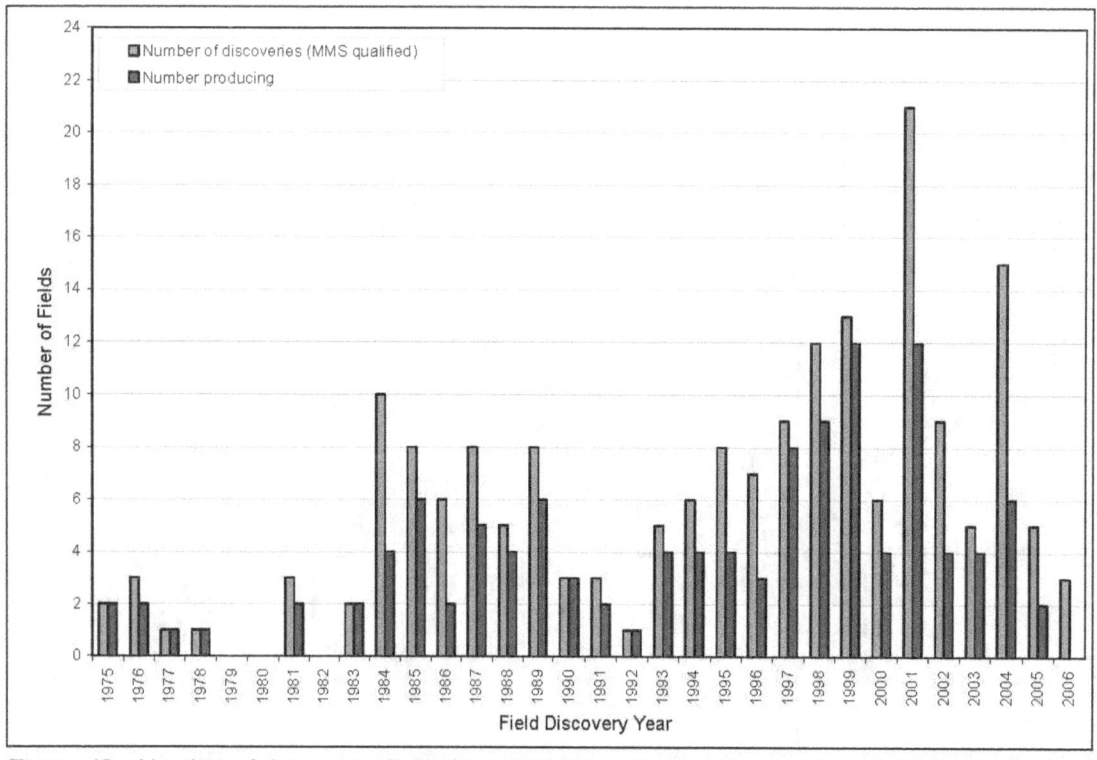

Figure 43. Number of deepwater field discoveries and the resulting number of producing fields.

In an attempt to capture the full impact of these deepwater exploratory successes, **Figure 44** adds MMS-known resource estimates and industry-announced discoveries to the proved and unproved reserve volumes. The industry-announced discovery volumes contain considerable uncertainty, are based on limited drilling, include numerous assumptions, and have not been confirmed by independent MMS analyses. They do, however, illustrate recent activity better than using only MMS proved reserve numbers. The apparent decline of proved reserve additions in recent years is caused by the previously mentioned developmental lag.

Figure 45 illustrate the distribution of recent hydrocarbon additions in the GOM, categorized by water depth. When comparing MMS proved reserve additions with those of the combination of unproved reserve estimates, known resources, and industry-announced deepwater discoveries, it can be seen that deepwater exploration has added significantly to the GOM hydrocarbon inventory. Last year, however, oil and gas reserves added to the GOM decreased sharply from those in 2006. This can be partially attributed to the smaller number and size of most of the announced discoveries in 2007, and the fact that MMS has not completed all reserve estimates for 2006 and 2007. These decreases are also likely to be the result of industry diverting its capital from exploration to appraisal and development.

PRODUCTION TRENDS

Leasing, drilling, and discoveries—all stepped into deeper waters with time. The final piece in the puzzle, production, is no exception. **Figure 46** illustrates deepwater projects that began production in 2006 and 2007 and those expected to commence production in the next 6 years. Ten deepwater projects went online in 2006 and another 15 in 2007, 9 of which were associated with the Independence Hub production facility. In addition to the projects shown in **Figure 46**, more are likely to come online in the next few years but are not shown because operators have not yet announced their plans. See **Appendix A** for a listing of all productive projects.

Table 6 shows that for the first time all of the 20 most prolific producing blocks in the GOM are located in deep water. **Figure 47** illustrates the relative volume of production from each GOM lease through time. Notice the large deepwater volumes that first appear in 1998 and 1999. More recent production continues to expand over a larger area and into deeper waters.

Figures 48a and 48b illustrate the importance of the GOM to the Nation's energy supply. The GOM supplied approximately 26 percent of the Nation's domestic oil and 15 percent of the Nation's domestic gas production in 2006. A significant portion of the oil volume came from the deep water. In fact, beginning in 2000, more oil has been produced from the deepwater areas of the GOM than from shallower waters. Total annual GOM gas contributions have slightly declined from 2005 to 2006. However, Independence Hub will add substantially to the Gulf's gas contributions in the near future. Production began in 2007, and when the project reaches full capacity of 1 billion cubic feet of gas per day, it will represent over 10 percent of the gas production from the GOM.

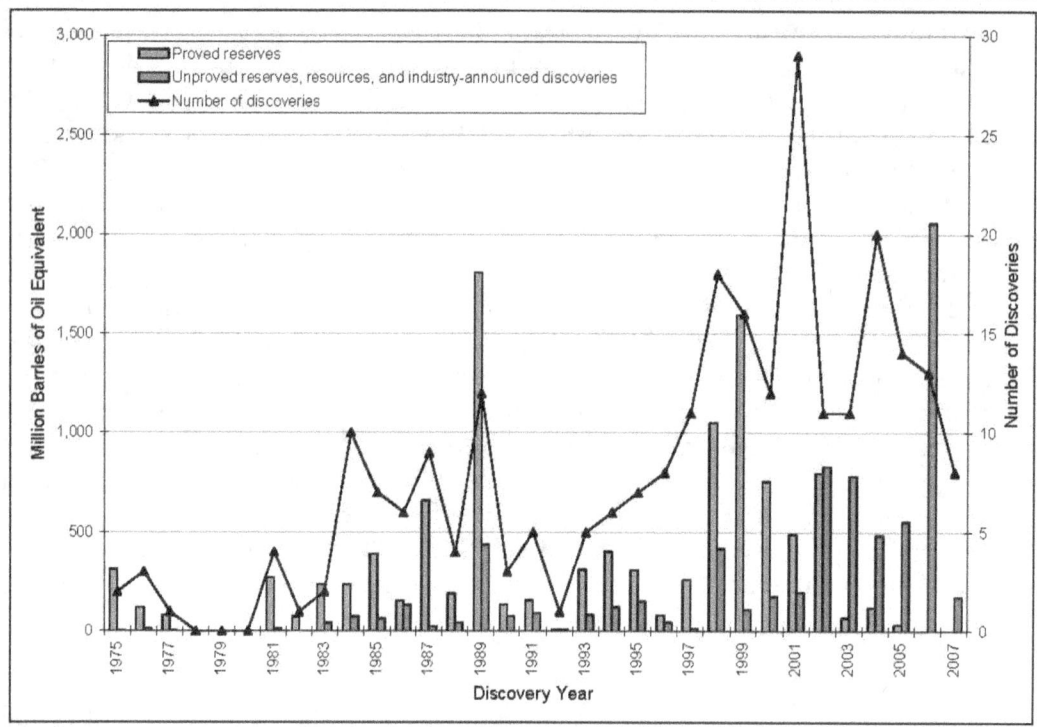

Figure 44. Number of deepwater field discoveries and new hydrocarbons found (MMS reserves, MMS resources, and industry-announced discoveries).

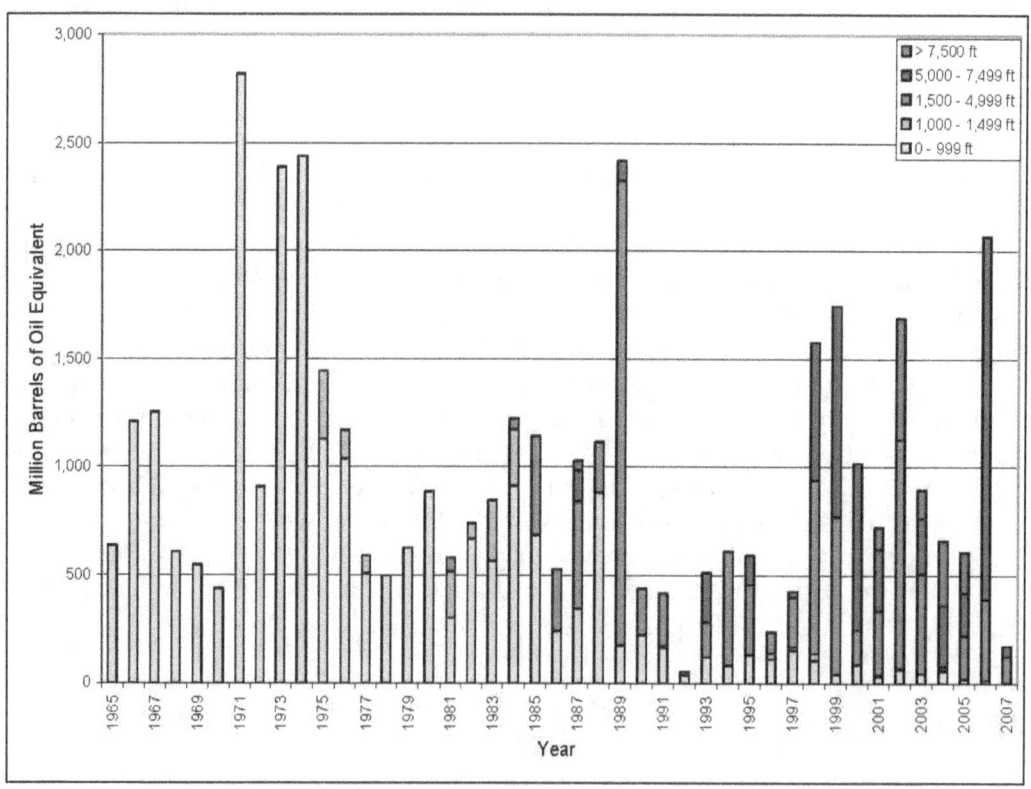

Figure 45. Barrels of oil equivalent added (reserves, known resources, and industry-announced discoveries).

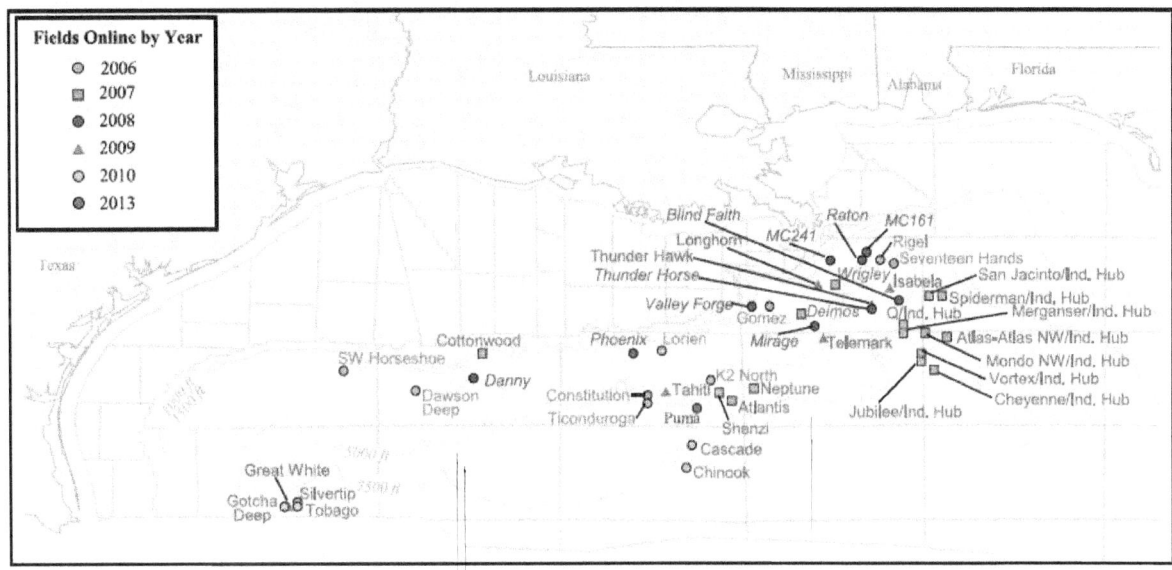

Figure 46. Deepwater projects that began production in 2006 and 2007 and those expected to begin production by yearend 2013.

Table 6. Top 20 Producing Blocks for the Years 2005-2006

Block	Project Name	Operator	Water Depth (ft)[1]	Production (BOE)[2]
MC 807	Mars	Shell	2,933	46,040,577
MC 383	Kepler (Na Kika)	BP	5,739	40,959,934
MC 809	Ursa	Shell	3,800	37,050,498
GC 644	Holstein	BP	4,340	27,076,950
MC 127	Horn Mountain	BP	5,400	23,957,778
GB 215	Conger	Amerada Hess	1,500	23,906,599
VK 786	Petronius	ChevronTexaco	1,753	23,187,217
MC 429	Ariel (Na Kika)	BP	6,240	23,105,523
GB 783	Magnolia	ConocoPhillips	4,670	22,792,615
GB 668	Gunnison	Kerr-McGee	3,126	22,558,126
VK 912	Ram-Powell	Shell	3,216	22,483,526
EB 602	Nansen	Kerr-McGee	3,580	21,889,299
MC 765	Princess	Shell	3,642	21,531,382
GC 782	Mad Dog	BP	4,420	21,164,896
MC 522	Fourier (Na Kika)	BP	6,940	18,707,968
MC 763	Mars	Shell	2,933	17,929,579
MC 85	King	BP	5,317	15,286,393
GB 385	Llano	Shell	2,610	13,097,959
MC 538	North Medusa	Murphy	2,095	12,989,679
MC 657	Coulomb (Na Kika)	Shell	7,565	12,975,899

BOE = barrels of oil equivalent   EB = East Breaks   GB = Garden Banks

GC = Green Canyon   MC = Mississippi Canyon   VK = Viosca Knoll

[1] Water depths are approximate and may vary depending on the location of the production facility or the location of a completed well (average of wells or deepest well site) in the block.

[2] Cumulative production from January 2005 through December 2006.

63

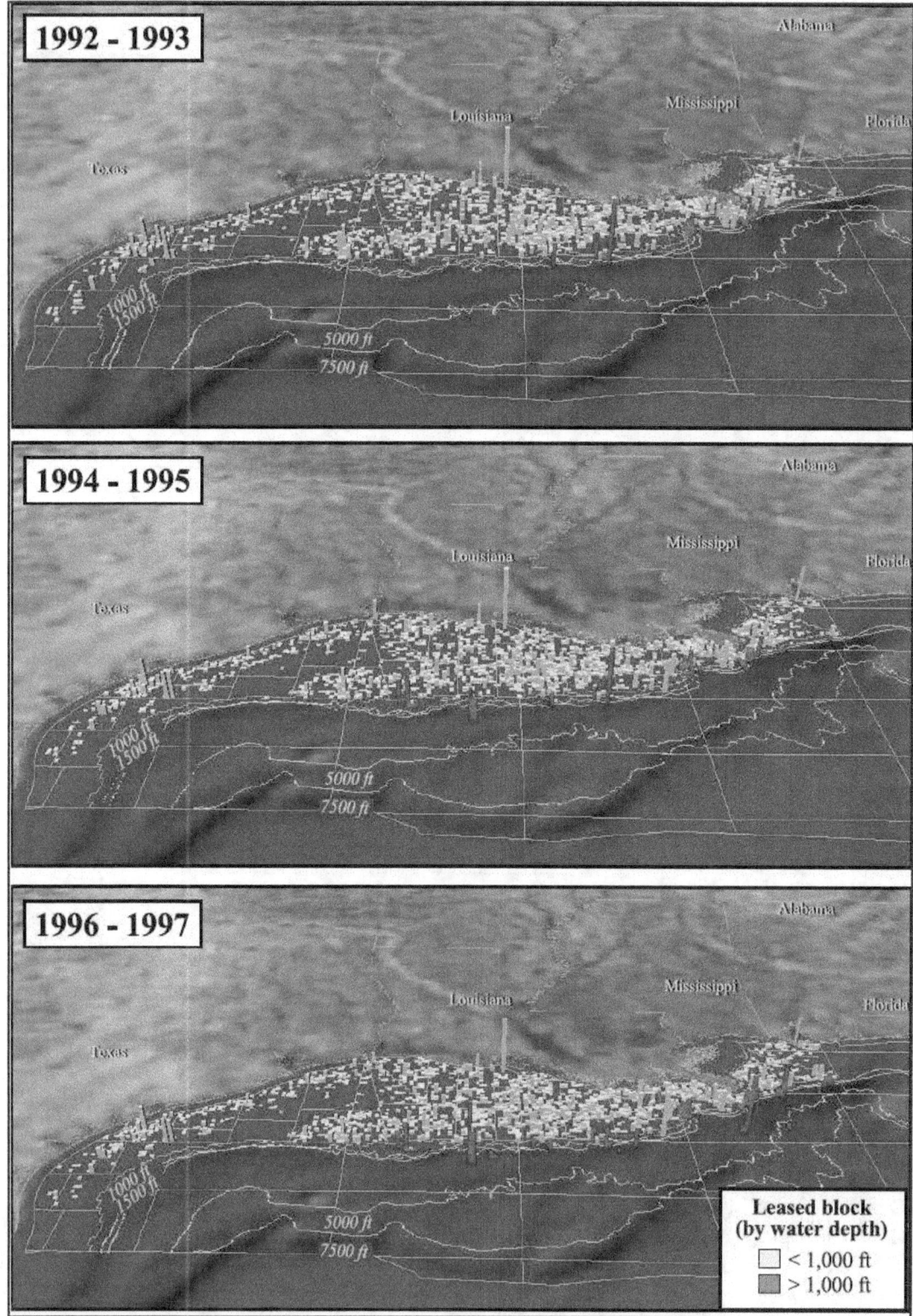

Figure 47. Relative volume of production from each Gulf of Mexico lease. (Bar heights are proportional to total lease production in barrels of oil equivalent during that interval.)

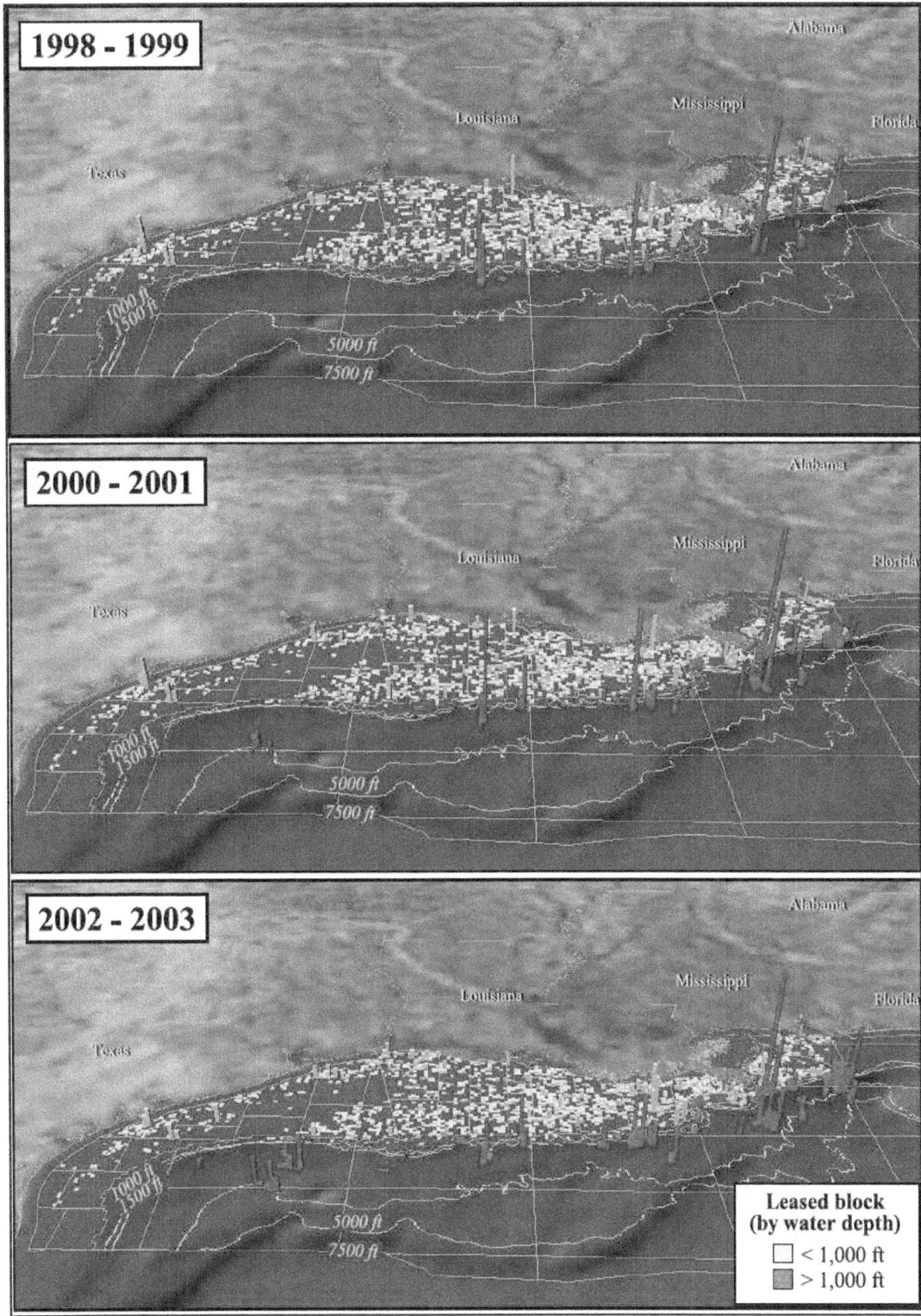

Figure 47. Relative volume of production from each Gulf of Mexico lease. (Bar heights are proportional to total lease production in barrels of oil equivalent during that interval.) (*continued*).

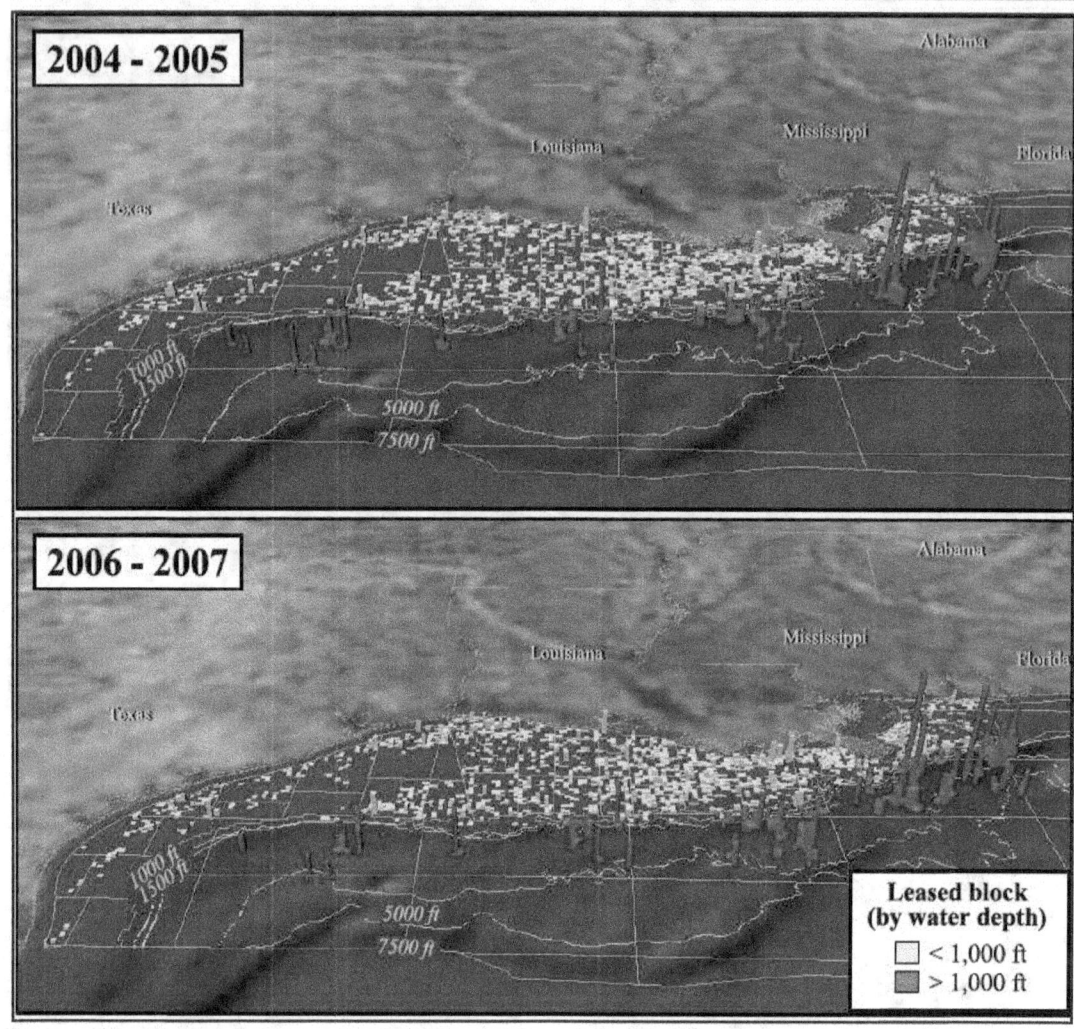

Figure 47.   Relative volume of production from each Gulf of Mexico lease. (Bar heights are proportional to total lease production in barrels of oil equivalent during that interval.) (continued).

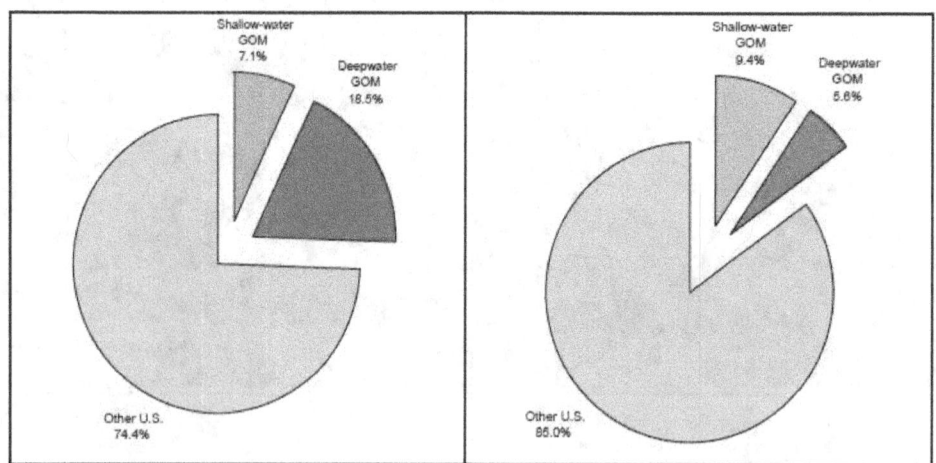

Figure 48a. Estimated U.S. oil production in 2006.

Figure 48b. Estimated U.S. gas production in 2006.

Figure 49a[3] illustrates historic trends in oil production. Shallow-water oil production rose rapidly in the 1960's, peaked in 1971, and has undergone cycles of increase and decline since then. Since 1997, the shallow-water GOM oil production has steadily declined and, at the end of 2006, was at its lowest level since 1965. From 1995 through 2003, deepwater oil production experienced a dramatic increase similar to that seen in the shallow-water GOM during the 1960's, offsetting declines in shallow-water oil production. Starting in 2003, deepwater oil production leveled off. In 2006, deepwater oil production accounted for over 72 percent of total GOM oil production. **Figure 49b** shows similar production trends for gas. Shallow-water gas production rose sharply throughout the 1960's and 1970's, and then remained relatively stable over the next 17 years before declining steadily from 1997 through today. At the same time shallow-water gas production started to decline in 1997, deepwater gas production began to increase, helping to offset the declines from shallow water. Gas production from deep water has, however, declined slightly from 2003 to the end of 2006. **Appendix D** lists historic GOM oil and gas production.

As discussed previously, the Deep Water Royalty Relief Act had a significant effect on deepwater leasing and drilling. Numerous projects with royalty-relief eligibility have come online in recent years (**Appendix A**), but the impact of the DWRRA on deepwater production began to show in 2002. Note that pre-DWRRA production refers to production from leases that have been approved to receive royalty relief but were issued before November 28, 1995. **Figure 50a** shows the contribution of deepwater royalty relief (DWRR) oil production to total "deepwater" GOM oil production, where "deepwater" is defined as 200 m (656 ft), the minimum water depth for which DWRR incentives are offered, instead of 1,000 ft (305 m), the definition used elsewhere in this report. Since the 2006 report (French et al., 2006), the amount of oil production subject to royalty suspension has slightly decreased. **Figure 50b** displays total "deepwater" gas production along with gas production subject to royalty relief. The volume of natural gas subject to royalty relief under the DWRRA increased rapidly in 2002, reaching its peak in 2005. Note that in these figures, pre-DWRRA production refers to production from leases that have been approved to receive royalty relief but were issued before November 28, 1995.

During 2006, approximately 300,000 barrels of oil and 1.4 billion cubic feet of gas came from deepwater subsea completions each day. Subsea completions currently account for about 30 percent of deepwater oil production and about 40 percent of deepwater gas production. **Figure 51a** shows that very little deepwater oil production came from subsea completions until mid-1995, after which subsea production generally increased until mid-2002. Since then, levels have decreased slightly and have remained relatively steady. Deepwater gas production from subsea completions began in mid-1993, generally increased until early-2004, and has subsequently decreased (**Figure 51b**).

---

[3] The dip in production in 2005 shown on this and some of the production graphics is the result of hurricane activity (Hurricanes Katrina and Rita). Production has quickly rebounded.

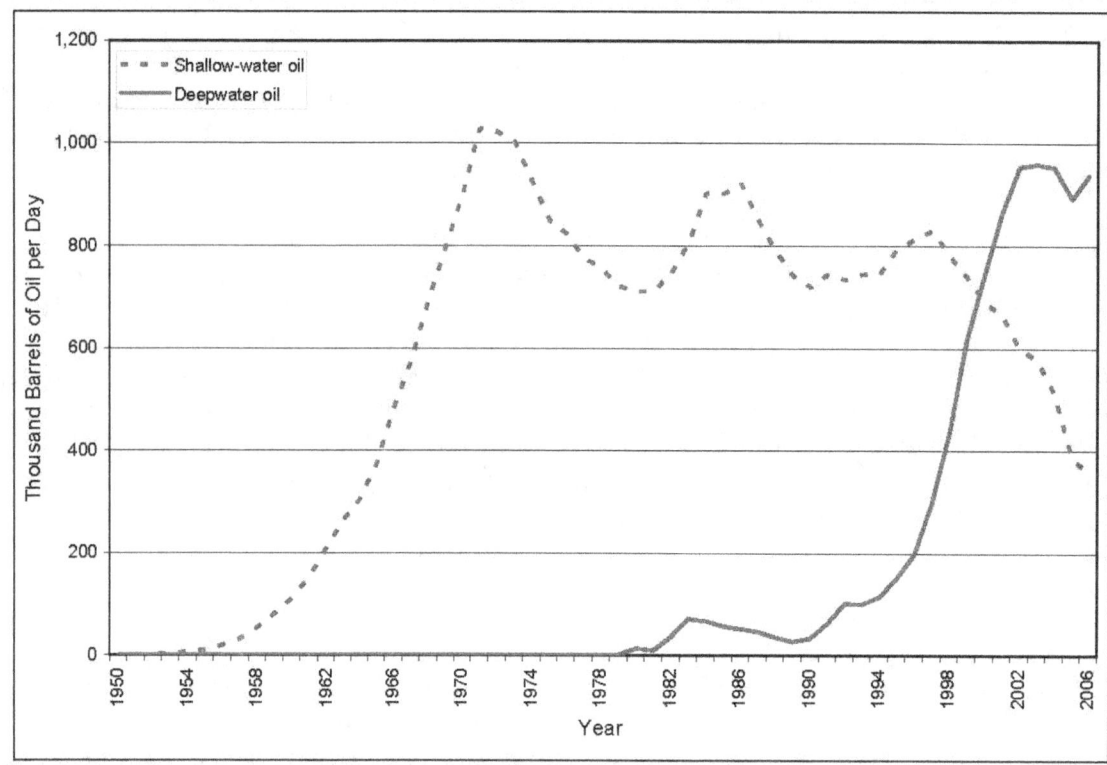

Figure 49a. Comparison of average annual shallow- and deepwater oil production.

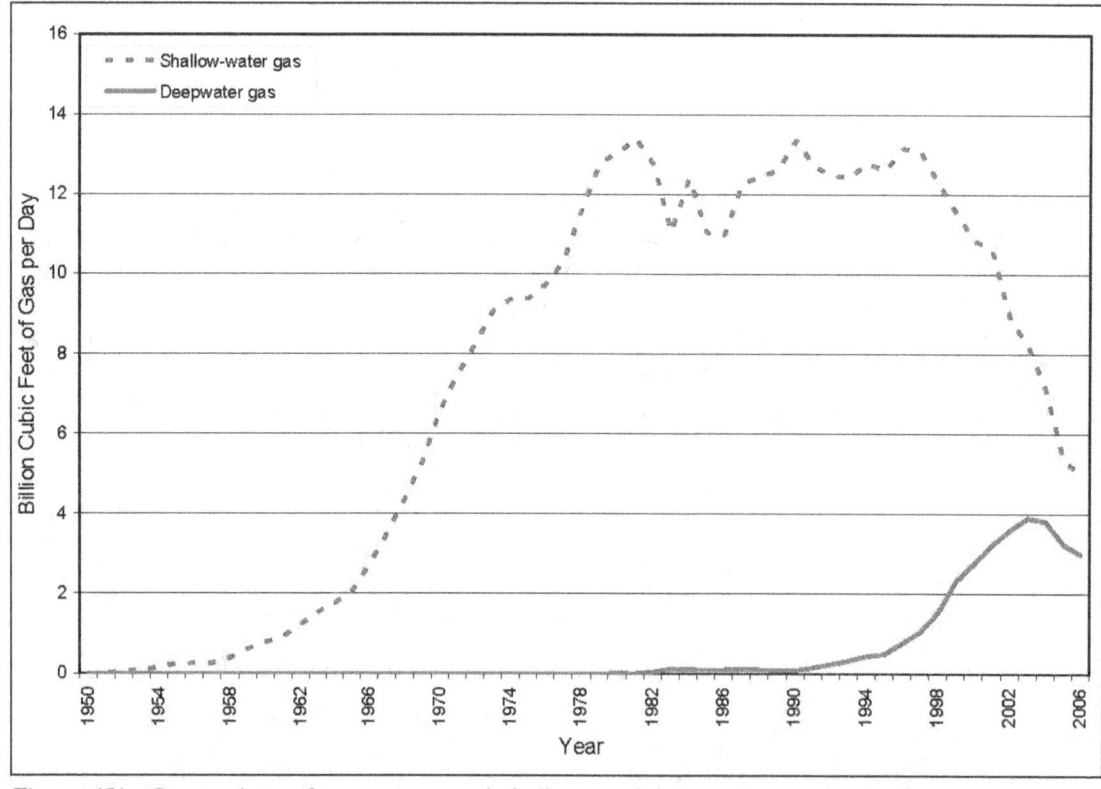

Figure 49b. Comparison of average annual shallow- and deepwater gas production.

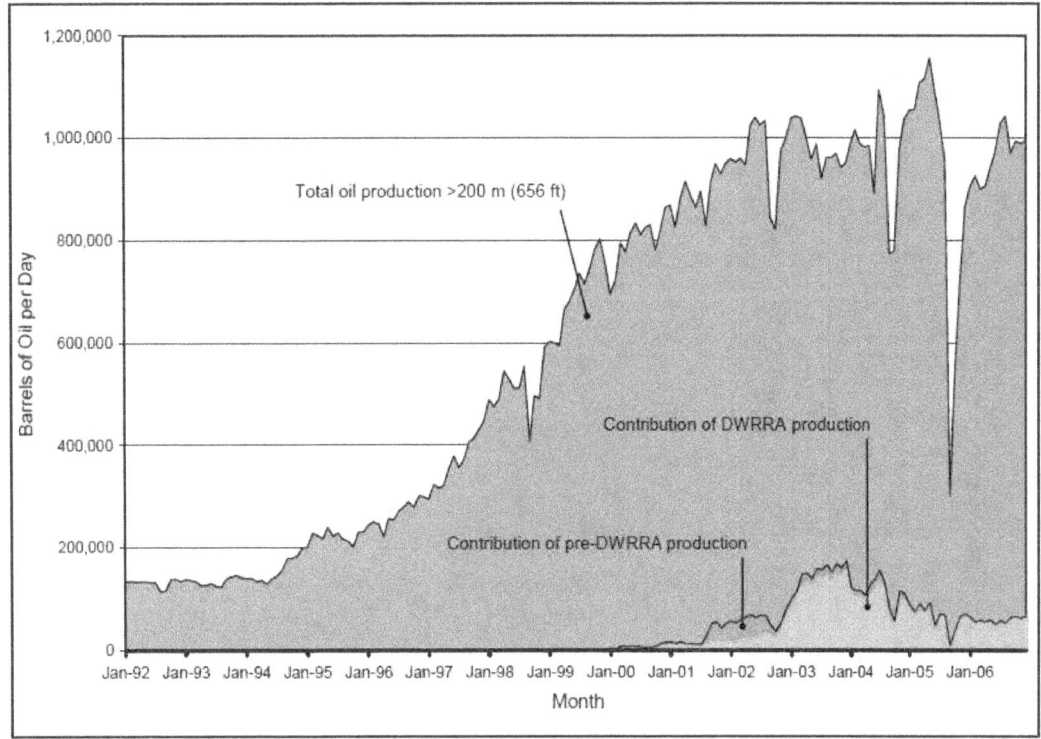

Figure 50a. Contribution of DWRRA oil production to total oil production in water depths greater than 200 m (656 ft).

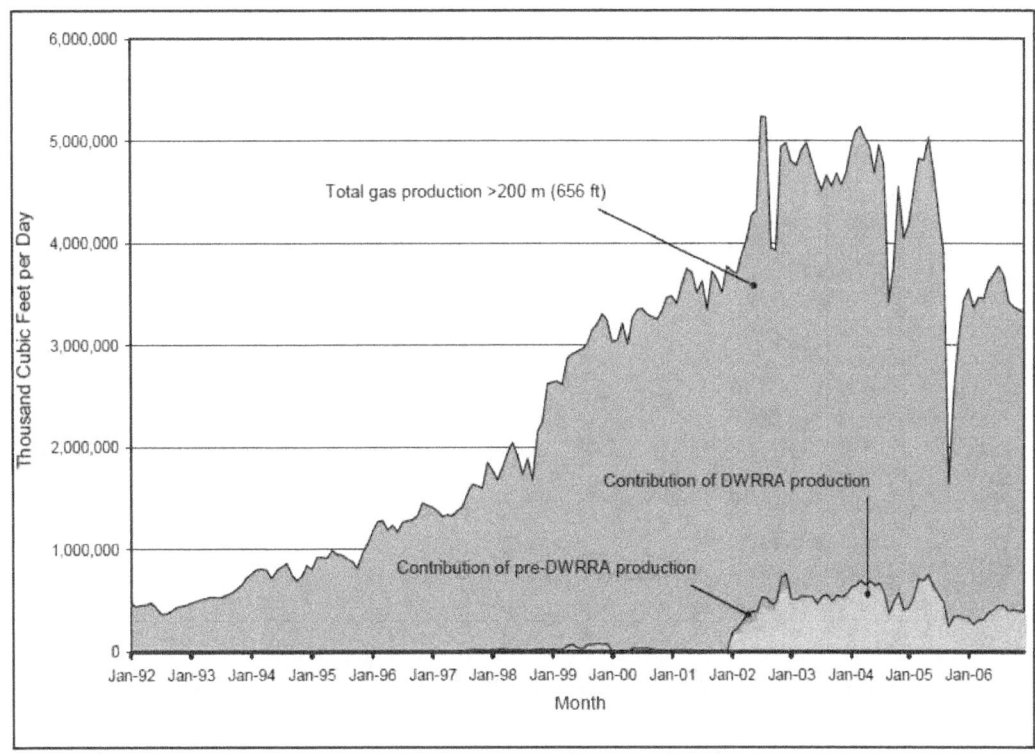

Figure 50b. Contribution of DWRRA gas production to total gas production in water depths greater than 200 m (656 ft).

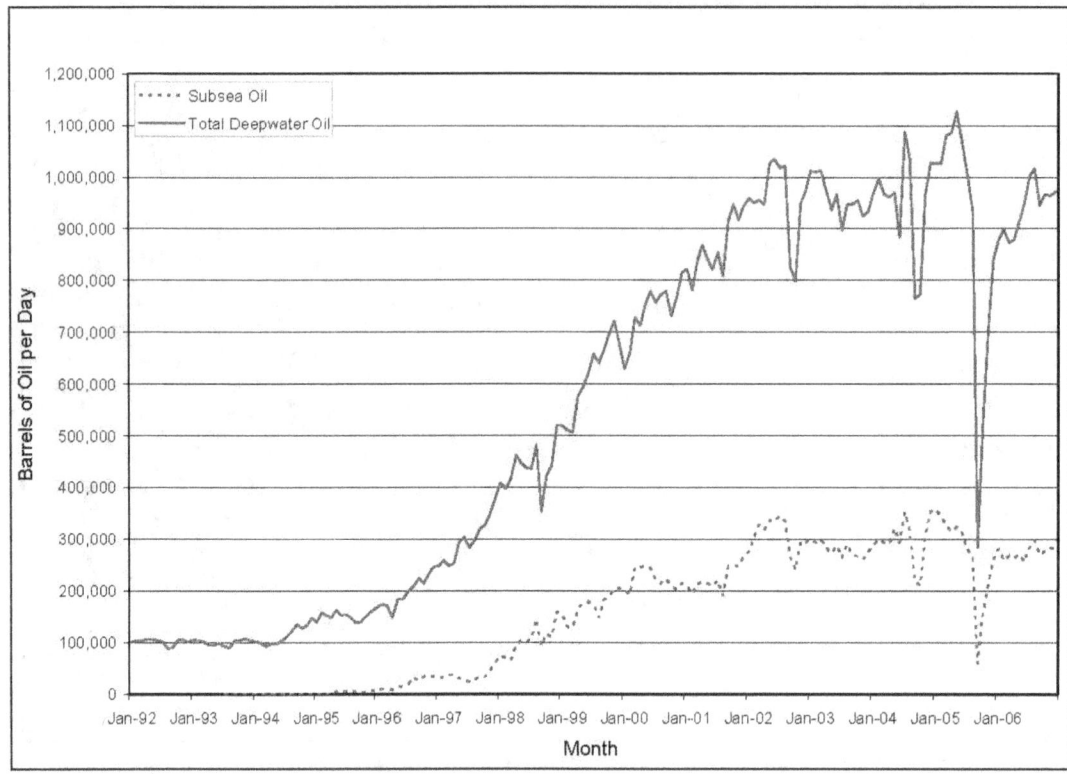

Figure 51a. Contributions from subsea completions toward total deepwater oil production.

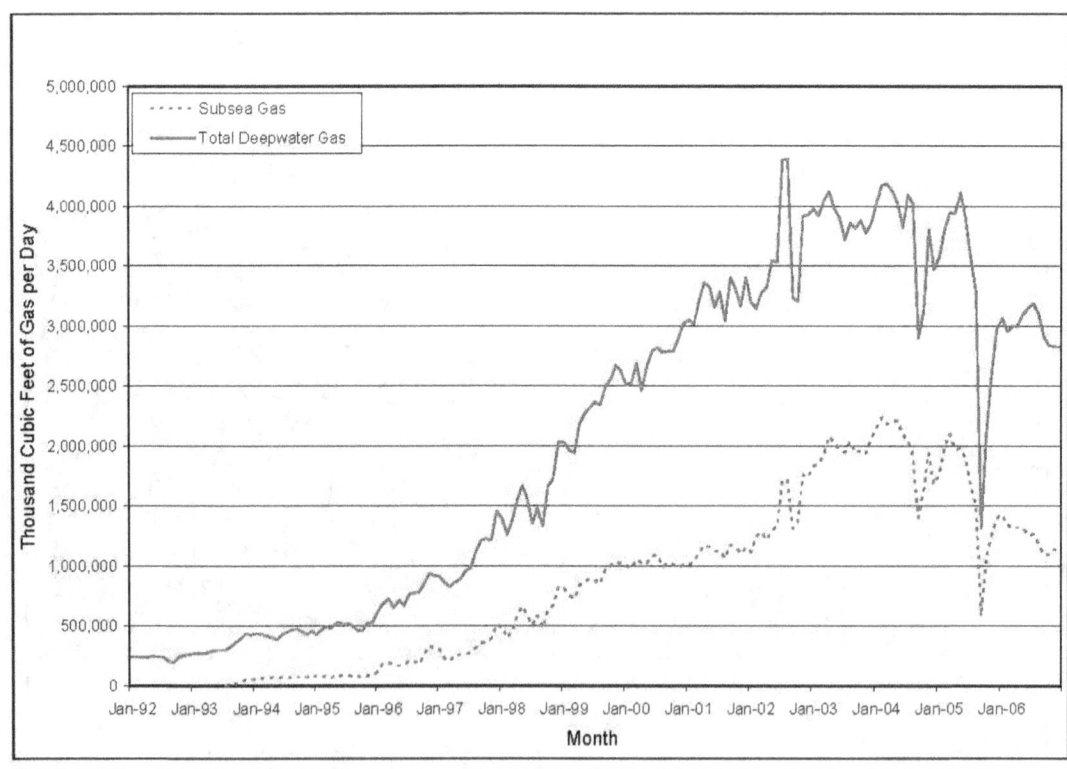

Figure 51b. Contributions from subsea completions toward total deepwater gas production.

PRODUCTION RATES

High well production rates have been a driving force behind the success of deepwater operations. **Figure 52a** illustrates the highest deepwater oil production rates for single wells (monthly production divided by actual production days). In the 1,500- to 4,999-ft (457- to 1,524-m) water depth interval, several large step increases have occurred as wells came online from fields such as Auger and Mars, culminating in a record maximum single well production rate of over 41,500 bo/d from Troika. After this time, major peaks have occurred for wells from Ursa and Brutus. In ultra-deep water, a Horn Mountain well established the record with over 32,000 bo/d in 2002. Wells at Kepler (Na Kika) came close to this record in 2005. **Figure 52b** shows maximum production rates for gas from single wells. In the 1,500- to 4,999-ft (457 to 1,524-m) water-depth interval, a well at Popeye set a record with over 143 MMcf/d in 1998. This record stood until 2002, when a single well at Mica surpassed this rate, with almost 145 MMcf/d. A single Mensa well holds the maximum gas production rate for the deepwater GOM at about 158,000 MMcf/d in 2004.

Figure 53a shows that the average deepwater oil completion currently produces at about 20 times the rate of the average shallow-water [less than 1,000 ft [305 m]] oil completion. The average deepwater gas completion currently produces at about 7 times the rate of the average shallow-water gas completion (**Figure 53b**). Deepwater oil production rates increased rapidly from 1996 through 1999 and remained relatively steady since that time. Deepwater gas production rates rose from 1996 to mid-1998, remaining relatively steady through 2004. It has declined overall since that time.

Figures 54a (oil) and **54b** (gas) compare maximum historic production rates for each lease in the GOM (i.e., the well with the highest historic production rate is shown for each lease). These maps show that many deepwater fields produce at some of the highest rates encountered in the GOM. **Figure 54a** also shows that maximum oil rates were significantly higher off the southeast Louisiana coast than off the Texas coast. Note that the pink bar in Walker Ridge is associated with the Jack #2 well test. **Figure 54b** illustrates the high deepwater gas production rates relative to the rest of the GOM. Some of the highest gas production rates are in Mississippi Canyon. Note also the excellent production rates from the Norphlet Trend (off the Alabama coast) and the Corsair Trend (off the Texas coast).

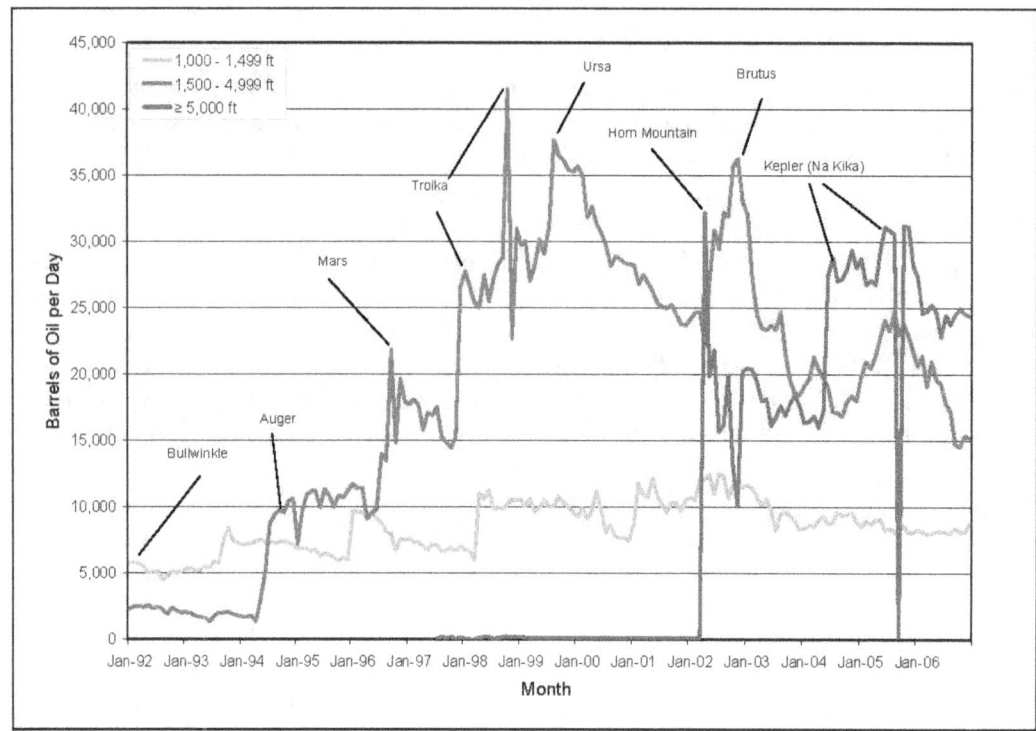

Figure 52a. Maximum production rates for a single well within each water-depth category for deepwater oil production.

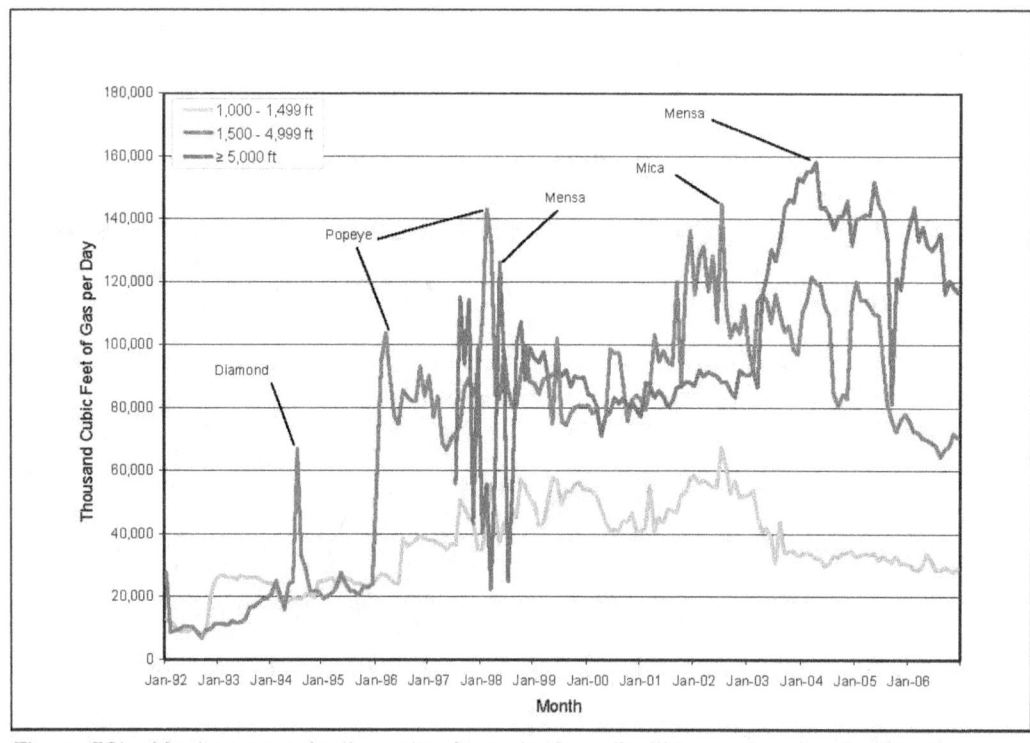

Figure 52b. Maximum production rates for a single well within each water-depth category for deepwater gas production.

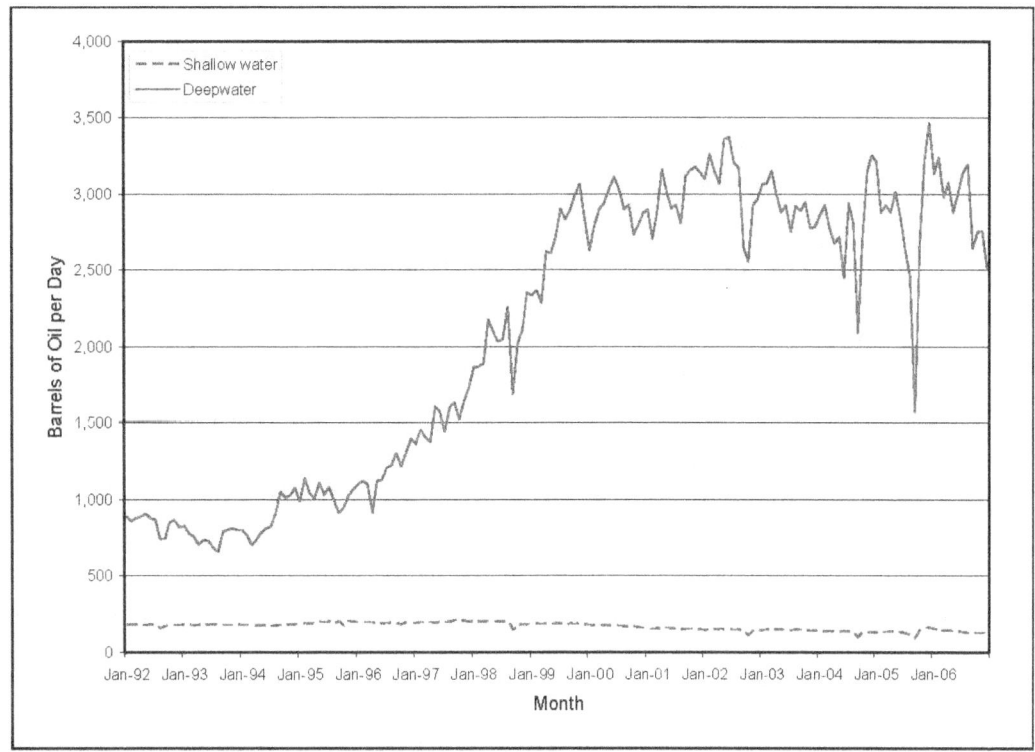

Figure 53a. Average production rates for shallow-water and deepwater oil well completions.

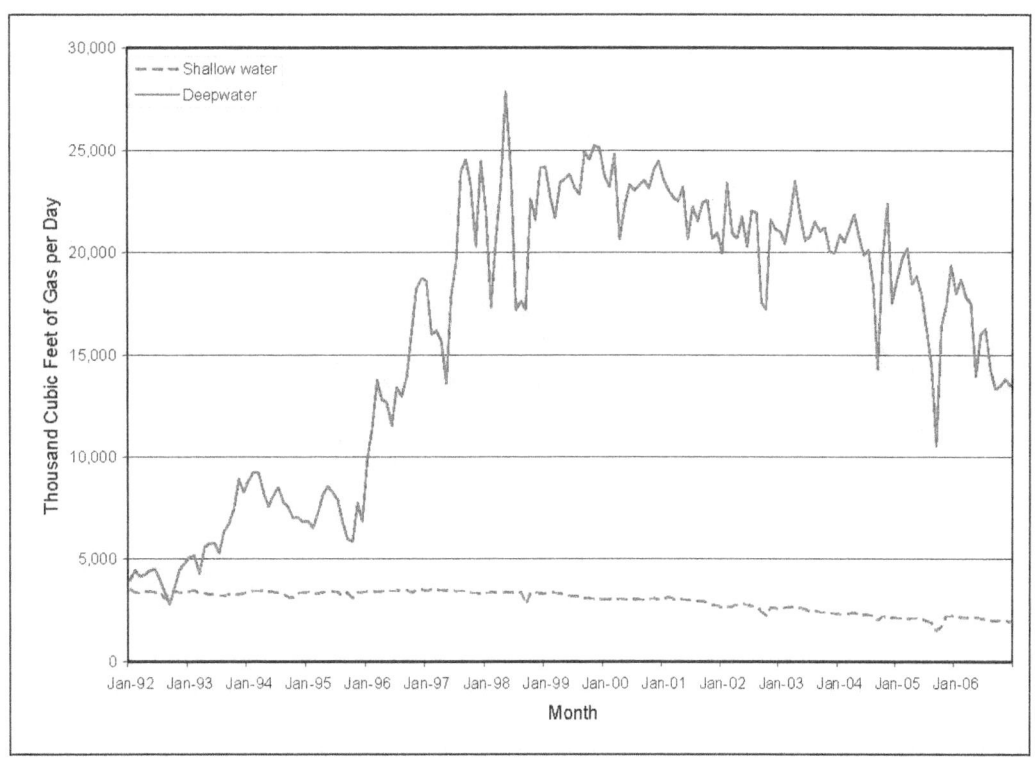

Figure 53b. Average production rates for shallow-water and deepwater gas well completions.

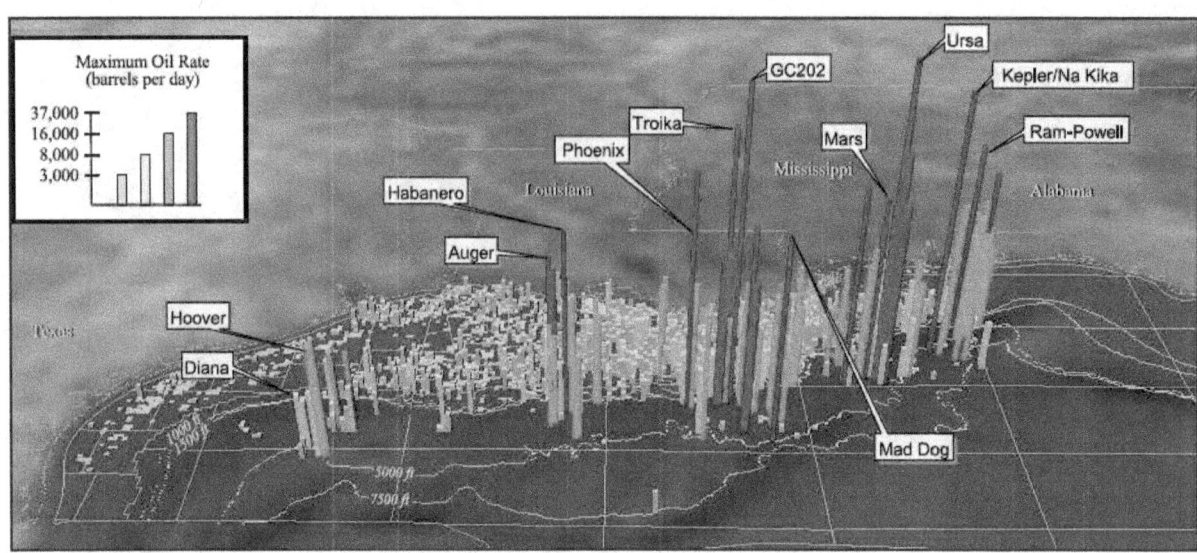

Figure 54a. Maximum historic oil production rates.

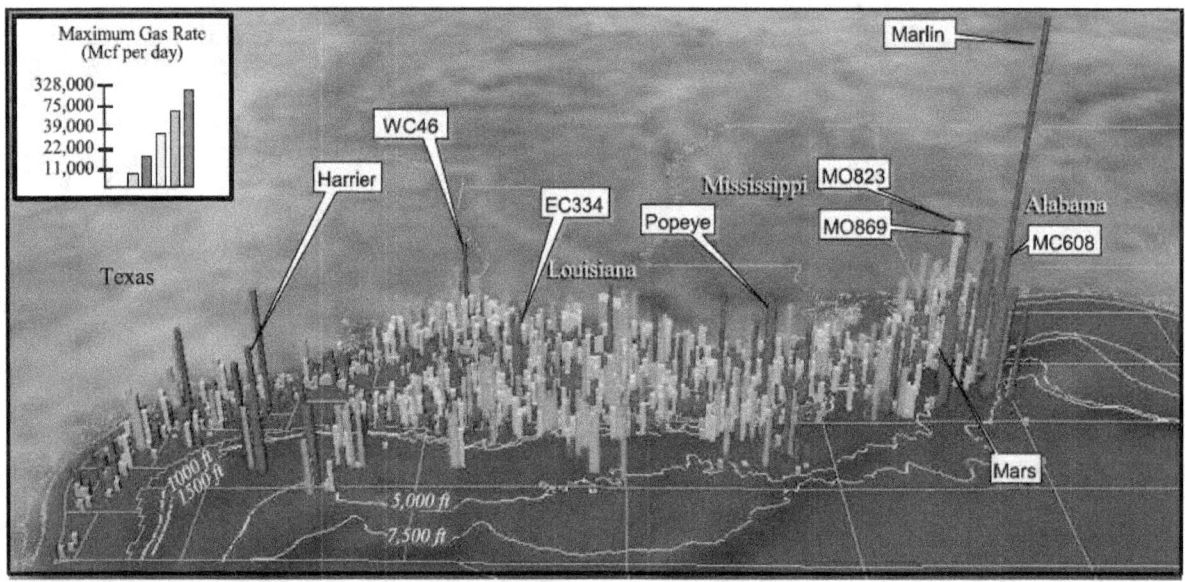

Figure 54b. Maximum historic gas production rates.

HIGHLIGHTS AND CONCLUSIONS

Highlights from this report include

- 54 percent of all GOM leases are located in deep water.

- Sale 206 attracted approximately $3.7 billion in high bids – the most since Federal offshore leasing began in 1954. The sum of the high bids for deepwater blocks was 93.2 percent of the total.

- Sale 224 was the first lease offering in the Eastern Gulf since 1988. This is also the first sale where the revenue sharing provisions of the Gulf of Mexico Energy Security Act of 2006 start immediately.

- Sale 205 was an exceptional lease offering that attracted over $2.9 billion in high bids on 723 blocks – the third largest total in U.S. offshore leasing history.

- A record high of 15 rigs were operating in ultra-deep water (≥5,000 ft or 1,524 m) in 2007.

- At least 13 new drilling rigs are being built and contracted for use in the ultra-deepwater Gulf and will be ready for operation in the next 2-3 years—they will be capable of operating in water depths up to 12,000 ft (3,658 m) and drilling up to 40,000 ft (12,192 m) in depth.

- There were eight industry-announced discoveries in 2007, including one in the Lower Tertiary.

- Of the 52 discoveries in ultra-deep water, Lower Tertiary rocks were encountered approximately 27 percent of the time.

- There are 125 proved deepwater fields in the GOM, representing a 44 percent increase since the end of 2006.

- Nonmajor companies have made more deepwater discoveries and hold more deepwater acreage than the major companies.

- There were 130 producing projects in the deepwater GOM at the end of 2007.

- For the first time, all of the 20 most prolific producing blocks in the GOM are located in deep water.

- Deepwater oil production rose about 820 percent and deepwater gas production increased about 1,155 percent from 1992 to 2006.

- Several fields associated with the Independence Hub production facility came online in 2007. When the hub is at full capacity, the gas production will represent over 10 percent of the total GOM gas production.

- Cheyenne, one of the subsea fields tying back to Independence Hub, has the deepest production in the GOM to date, in a water depth of 8,960 ft (2,731 m).

- The first FPSO for use in the U.S. GOM will be installed for the development of the Cascade and Chinook Fields in Walker Ridge, with first oil expected in 2010.

- Another first for the GOM will be the installation of a ship-shape, dynamically positioned, disconnectable turret FPU for the Phoenix development in Green Canyon, with a planned production startup in the third quarter of 2008.

- The Perdido Regional Development hub will produce the Great White, Tobago and Silvertip discoveries in Alaminos Canyon beginning in 2010. Once installed, the truss spar will set a new record as the deepest spar in over 8,000 ft (2,438 m) of water depth.

- The Atlantis semisubmersible platform in the deepwater GOM is the deepest moored, floating oil and gas production facility in the world.

- Deepwater subsea wells constitute 63 percent of the total subsea well population in the GOM.

The future of deepwater GOM exploration and production remains very promising. Factors contributing to the increase in deepwater activity include several key discoveries (including those recent discoveries in the Lower Tertiary Trend), the recognition of high production rates, the evolution of development technologies, and a rise in oil and gas prices.

The remainder of this report combines historic leasing, drilling, development, reserve, and production data, revealing overall trends in deepwater activity and expectations.

DEVELOPMENT CYCLE

There is often a considerable lag between leasing and first production. These lags are not unusual with complex deepwater developments. **Figure 55** demonstrates average lags associated with deepwater operations. This figure uses data from only productive deepwater leases and illustrates the lags between leasing and qualification and from qualification to first production. Operators sometimes announce discoveries to the public long before qualifying the lease as productive with MMS (and thereby granted field status). Note that, since deepwater leases are in effect for 8 or 10 years, the data are incomplete beyond 1997. The decreasing lags for leases issued after 1997 are partially the result of continued lease evaluation by industry and subsea tiebacks to existing hubs.

Figure 55 indicates that, as industry gains experience in the deepwater areas of the Gulf, the time between leasing and production is reduced. Noteworthy is the reduction in time from lease acquisition to first well drilled from the 1980's to the 1990's. Developments near accessible infrastructure and the use of proven development technologies can also reduce the lag between leasing and production. However, as new discoveries move into dramatically deeper water depths, and with many new discoveries being far from existing infrastructure, an increase in lag time between leasing and production should be anticipated. Conditions such as high temperature and high pressure in wells will complicate drilling and development operations, resulting in longer lags as well.

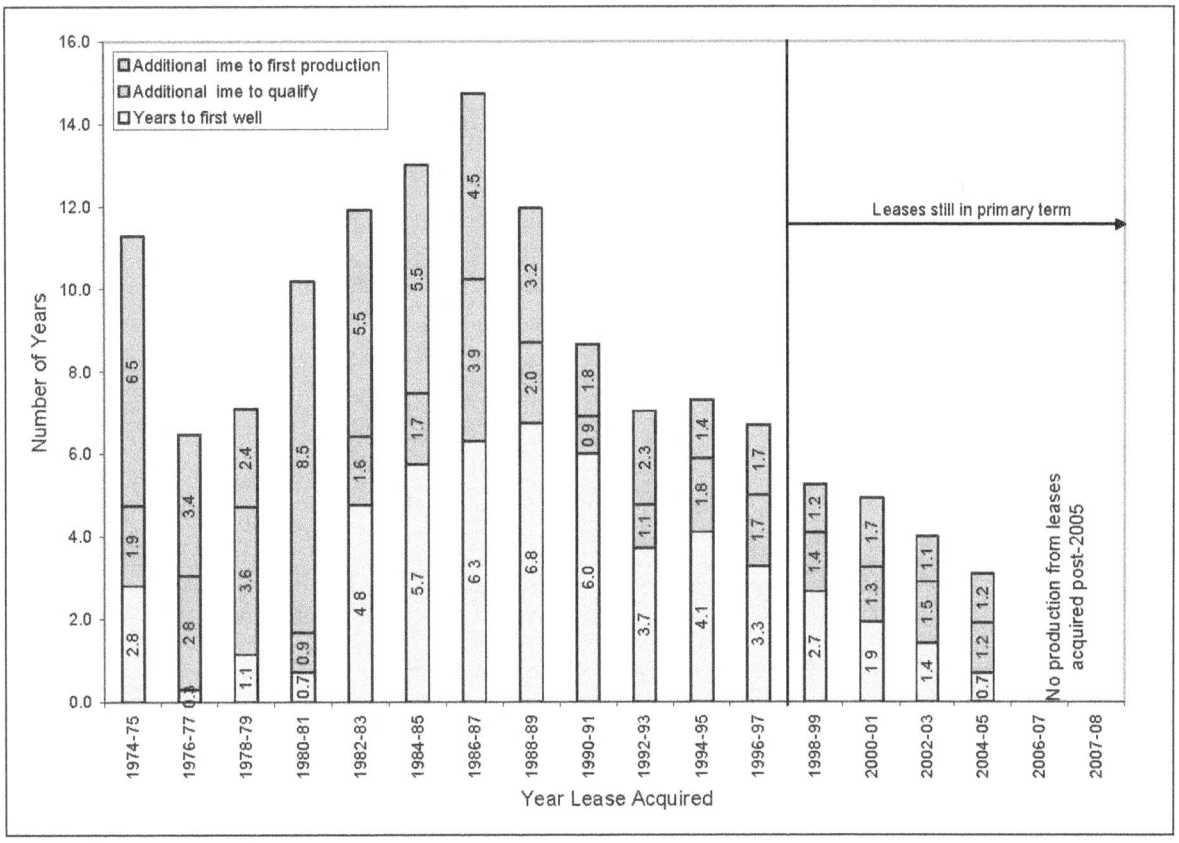

Figure 55. Lag from leasing to first production for producing deepwater fields.

DRILLING THE LEASE INVENTORY

Figure 56 illustrates the magnitude of the deepwater lease inventory and industry's ability to evaluate this large number of leases. The annual historic lease data from 1984 through 2007 are indicated by the solid colored lines and depict the number of active leases, the number of leases drilled, and the number of leases expiring undrilled. Future projected values for expiring leases and leases drilled are depicted in the dotted lines. These projected values assume that, after the year 2007, all leases will expire unless drilled and that 60 untested deepwater leases will be drilled each year.

Of the deepwater leases acquired in the 1996-2007 sales, over 3,700 are still active, with more than 1,870 of these active leases located in ultra-deep water ($\geq$5,000 ft or $\geq$1,524 m). Only 272 wells have been drilled on 124 ultra-deepwater leases from these sales; 47 of these resulted in announced discoveries. The available deepwater drilling rig fleet, even with its projected additions, will challenge industry's ability to evaluate their lease inventory.

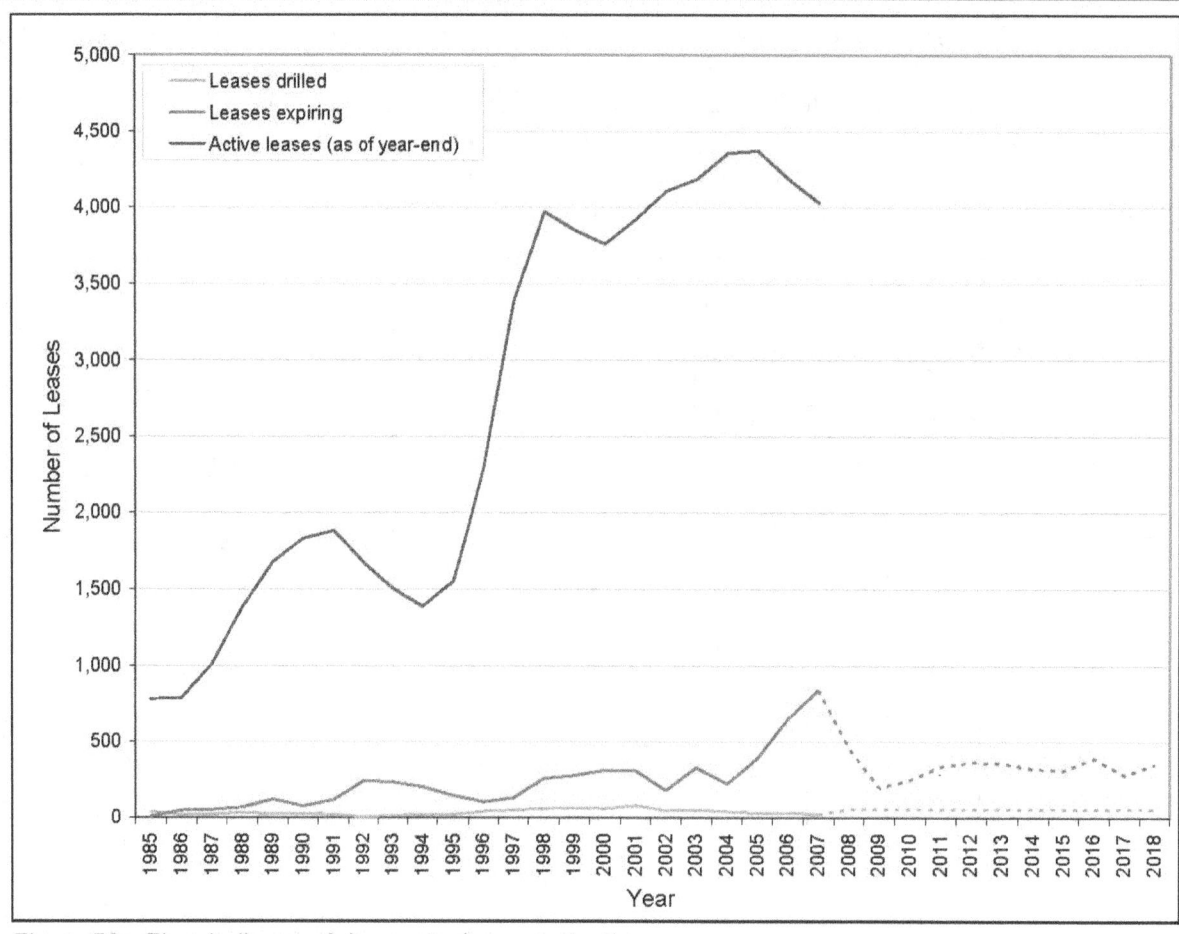

Figure 56.   The challenge of deepwater lease evaluation.

Other factors play a significant role in the industry's ability to evaluate their GOM lease inventory, including alternative deepwater exploration and development targets throughout the world, capital limitations, and limited qualified personnel.

AMERICA'S OFFSHORE ENERGY FUTURE

The deepwater GOM will play an important part in the Nation's future energy supply. A large inventory of active deepwater leases is available to the industry for exploration. Traditional deepwater minibasin plays, and new ultra-deepwater plays near and even beyond the Sigsbee Escarpment, beneath thick salt canopies, and in lightly explored Lower Tertiary reservoirs are all being actively explored and developed. New technology is also advancing to facilitate ultra-deepwater activities. Likewise, growth in deepwater infrastructure will occur. All of these factors will ensure that the deepwater GOM will remain one of the world's premier oil and gas basins.

CONTRIBUTING PERSONNEL

This report includes contributions from the following individuals:

Pat Adkins

Kim Altobelli

Pat Bryars

Carole Current

Eric Hawkins

Jack Irion

Stephen Kovacs

Deborah Miller

Stephen Pomes

Mike Prendergast

Terry Rankin

Bill Shedd

REFERENCES

American Petroleum Institute (API). In preparation. Recommended Practice API RP 17 O, High Integrity Pressure Protection Systems (HIPPS). Washington, DC: American Petroleum Institute.

Atauz, A.D., W. Bryant, T. Jones, and B. Phaneuf. 2006. Mica shipwreck project: Deepwater archaeological investigation of a 19th century shipwreck in the Gulf of Mexico. U.S. Dept. of the Interior, Minerals Management Service, Gulf of Mexico OCS Region, New Orleans, LA. OCS Study MMS 2006-072. 116 pp. Internet website: http://www.gomr.mms.gov/PI/PDFImages/ESPIS/4/4216.pdf

Church, R., D. Warren, R. Cullimore, L. Johnston, W. Schroeder, W. Patterson, T. Shirley, M. Kilgour, N. Morris, and J. Moore. 2007. Archaeological and biological analysis of World War II shipwrecks in the Gulf of Mexico: Artificial reef effect in deep water. U.S. Dept. of the Interior, Minerals Management Service, Gulf of Mexico OCS Region, New Orleans, LA. OCS Study MMS 2007-015. 387 pp. Internet website: http://www.gomr.mms.gov/PI/PDFImages/ESPIS/4/4239.pdf

Collett, T.S. 1995. Gas hydrate resources of the United States. In: Gautier, D.L., G.L. Dolton, K.L. Takahashi, and K.L. Varnes, eds. 1995 National assessment of United States oil and gas resources. On CD-ROM: U.S. Dept. of the Interior, Geological Survey. U.S. Geological Survey Digital Data Series 30.

Cranswick, D. and J. Regg. 1997. Deepwater in the Gulf of Mexico: America's new frontier. U.S. Dept. of the Interior, Minerals Management Service, Gulf of Mexico OCS Region, New Orleans, LA. OCS Report MMS 97-0004. 41 pp.

Crawford, T.G., G.L. Burgess, C.J. Kinler, M.T. Prendergast, K.M. Ross, and N.K Shepard. 2006. *Estimated* oil and gas reserves, Gulf of Mexico, December 31, 2003. U.S. Dept. of the Interior, Minerals Management Service, Gulf of Mexico OCS Region, New Orleans, LA. OCS Report MMS 2006-069. 48 pp.

Donohue, K., P. Hamilton, K. Leaman, R. Leben, M. Prater, D.R. Watts, and E. Waddell. 2006a. Exploratory study of deepwater currents in the Gulf of Mexico. Volume I: Executive summary. U.S. Dept. of the Interior, Minerals Management Service, Gulf of Mexico OCS Region, New Orleans, LA. OCS Study MMS 2006-073. 86 pp.

Donohue, K., P. Hamilton, K. Leaman, R. Leben, M. Prater, D.R. Watts, and E. Waddell. 2006b. Exploratory study of deepwater currents in the Gulf of Mexico. Volume II: Technical report. U.S. Dept. of the Interior, Minerals Management Service, Gulf of Mexico OCS Region, New Orleans, LA. OCS Study MMS 2006-074. 430 pp.

Federal Register. 2006. Federal Outer Continental Shelf (OCS) administrative boundaries extending from the Submerged Lands Act boundary seaward to the limit of the United States Outer Continental Shelf. Tuesday, January 3, 2006. 71 FR 1, pp. 127-131.

Federal Register. 2008a. Outer Continental Shelf (OCS) Central Gulf of Mexico (GOM) Planning Area Oil and Gas Lease Sale 206: Final Notice of Sale, Wednesday, February 13, 2008. 73 FR 30, pp. 8347-8353.

Federal Register. 2008b. Outer Continental Shelf (OCS) Eastern Gulf of Mexico (GOM) Planning Area Oil and Gas Lease Sale 224: Final Notice of Sale, Wednesday, February 13, 2008. 73 FR 30, pp. 8353-8355.

French, L.S., G.E. Richardson, E.G. Kazanis, T.M. Montgomery, C.M. Bohannon, and M.P. Gravois. 2006. Deepwater Gulf of Mexico 2006: America's expanding frontier. U.S. Dept. of the Interior, Minerals Management Service, Gulf of Mexico OCS Region, New Orleans, LA. OCS Report MMS 2006-022. 144 pp.

Hamilton, P., T.J. Berger, J.J. Singer, E. Waddell, J.H. Churchill, R.R. Leben, T.N. Lee, and W. Sturges. 2000. DeSoto Canyon eddy intrusion study: Final report. Volume II: Technical report. U.S. Dept of the Interior, Minerals Management Service, Gulf of Mexico OCS Region, New Orleans, LA. OCS Study MMS 2000-80. 275 pp.

Hamilton, P., J.J. Singer, E. Waddell, and K. Donohue. 2003. Deepwater observations in the northern Gulf of Mexico from in-situ current meters and PIES. Volume II: Technical report. U.S. Dept. of the Interior, Minerals Management Service, Gulf of Mexico OCS Region, New Orleans, LA. OCS Report MMS 2003-049. 95 pp.

Hegna, S. and D. Gaus. 2003. Improved imaging by pre-stack depth migration of multi-azimuth towed streamer seismic data. 65th European Association of Geoscientists & Engineers Conference and Exhibition. Expanded abstracts. C02.

Howard, M.S. 2004. Rich azimuth marine acquisition. European Association of Geoscientists & Engineers Research Workshop: Advances in Seismic Acquisition Technology. Rhodes, Greece.

Kapoor, J., M. Moldevaneau, M. Egan, M O'Briain, D. Desta, I. Atakishiyev, M. Tomida, and L. Stewart. 2007. Subsalt imaging: The RAZ-WAZ experience. The Leading Edge. 26(11):1414-1422.

Kempthorne, D. 2007. Kempthorne may offer areas in the North Aleutian Basin, Central Gulf of Mexico for leasing; increase royalty rate for offshore oil and gas leases. Press Release, January 9, 2007. Washington, DC. Internet website: http://www.mms.gov/ooc/press/2007/pressdoi0109.htm

Lugo-Fernández, A., D.A. Ball, M. Gravois, C. Horrell, and J.B. Irion. 2007. Analysis of the Gulf of Mexico's Veracruz-Havana route of *La Flota de la Nueva España.* Journal of Maritime Archaeology 2:24-47.

O'Connell, J., M. Kohli, and S. Amos. 1993. Bullwinkle: A unique 3-D experiment. *Geophysics.* 58:167-176.

Peterson, R.H., G.E. Richardson, C.M. Bohannon, E.G. Kazanis, T.M. Montgomery, L.D. Nixon, M.P. Gravois, and G.D. Klocek. 2007. Deepwater Gulf of Mexico 2007: Interim report of 2006 highlights. U.S. Dept. of the Interior, Minerals Management Service, Gulf of Mexico OCS Region, New Orleans, LA. OCS Report MMS 2007-021. 74 pp.

Rivas, D., A. Badan, and J. Ochoa. 2005. The ventilation of the deep Gulf of Mexico. Journal of Physical Oceanography. 35: 1763-1781.

Rivas, D., A. Badan, J. Sheinbaum, J. Ochoa, and J. Candela. In review. Vertical velocity and vertical heat flux observed within Loop Current eddies in the central Gulf of Mexico. Journal of Physical Oceanography.

Sheinbaum J., A. Badan, J. Ochoa, J. Candela, D. Rivas, and J.I. González. 2007. Full-water column current observations in the central Gulf of Mexico. U.S. Dept. of the Interior, Minerals Management Service, Gulf of Mexico OCS Region, New Orleans, LA. OCS Study MMS 2007-022. xiv + 58 pp.

Sturges, W. 2005. Deep-water exchange between the Atlantic, Caribbean and Gulf of Mexico. In: Sturges, W. and A. Lugo-Fernandez, eds. Circulation in the Gulf of Mexico: Observations and models. American Geophysical Union Monograph No. 161. Pp. 263-278.

Sukup, D.V. 2002. Wide-azimuth marine acquisition by the Helix Method. The Leading Edge 21(8):791-794.

U.S. Dept. of the Interior, Minerals Management Service. 2000. Deepwater Gulf of Mexico OCS currents. U.S. Dept. of the Interior, Minerals Management Service, Gulf of Mexico OCS Region, New Orleans, LA. MMS Safety Alert Notice No. 180.

U.S. Dept. of the Interior, Minerals Management Service. 2003. Exploration activities in the eastern sale area: Eastern Planning Area, Gulf of Mexico OCS: Programmatic environmental assessment. U.S. Dept. of the Interior, Minerals Management Service, Gulf of Mexico OCS Region, New Orleans, LA. OCS EIS/EA MMS 2003-008. 201 pp.

U.S. Dept. of the Interior, Minerals Management Service. 2007. Deepwater ocean current monitoring on floating facilities. U.S. Dept. of the Interior, Minerals Management Service, Gulf of Mexico OCS Region, New Orleans, LA. NTL 2007-G17.

U.S. Dept. of the Interior, Minerals Management Service. 2008. Preliminary evaluation of in-place hydrate resources: Gulf of Mexico Outer Continental Shelf. Compiled by Matthew Frye. U.S. Dept. of the Interior, Minerals Management Service, Gulf of Mexico OCS Region, New Orleans, LA. OCS Report MMS 2008-004. 136 pp.

APPENDICES

APPENDIX A. DEVELOPMENT SYSTEMS OF PRODUCTIVE DEEPWATER PROJECTS

Year of First Production	Project Name[3]	Operator	Block	Water Depth (ft)[4]	System Type	DWRR[5]
1979	Cognac	Shell	MC 194	1,023	Fixed Platform	
1984	Lena	ExxonMobil	MC 280	1,000	Compliant Tower	
1988[1]	GC 29	Placid	GC 29	1,540	Semisubmersible/ Subsea	
1988[1]	GC 31	Placid	GC 31	2,243	Subsea	
1989	Bullwinkle	Shell	GC 65	1,353	Fixed Platform	
1989	Jolliet	ConocoPhillips	GC 184	1,760	TLP	
1991	Amberjack	BP	MC 109	1,100	Fixed Platform	
1992	Alabaster	ExxonMobil	MC 485	1,438	Subsea	
1993[1]	Diamond	Kerr-McGee	MC 445	2,095	Subsea	
1993	Zinc	ExxonMobil	MC 354	1,478	Subsea	
1994	Auger	Shell	GB 426	2,860	TLP	
1994	Pompano/Pompano II	BP	VK 989	1,290	Fixed Platform/ Subsea	
1994	Tahoe/SE Tahoe	Shell	VK 783	1,500	Subsea	
1995[2]	Cooper	Newfield	GB 388	2,097	Semisubmersible	
1995[1]	Shasta	ChevronTexaco	GC 136	1,048	Subsea	
1995	VK 862	Walter	VK 862	1,043	Subsea	
1996	Mars	Shell	MC 807	2,933	TLP/Subsea	
1996	Popeye	Shell	GC 116	2,000	Subsea	
1996[1]	Rocky	Shell	GC 110	1,785	Subsea	
1997	Mensa	Shell	MC 731	5,318	Subsea	
1997	Neptune	Kerr-McGee	VK 826	1,930	Spar/Subsea	
1997	Ram-Powell	Shell	VK 956	3,216	TLP	
1997	Troika	BP	GC 200	2,721	Subsea	
1998	Arnold	Marathon	EW 963	1,800	Subsea	
1998	Baldpate	Amerada Hess	GB 260	1,648	Compliant Tower	
1998	Morpeth	Eni	EW 921	1,700	TLP/Subsea	
1998	Oyster	Marathon	EW 917	1,195	Subsea	
1999	Allegheny	Eni	GC 254	3,294	TLP	
1999	Angus	Shell	GC 113	2,045	Subsea	
1999[1]	Dulcimer	Mariner	GB 367	1,120	Subsea	Yes

Year of First Production	Project Name[3]	Operator	Block	Water Depth (ft)[4]	System Type	DWRR[5]
1999	EW 1006	Walter	EW 1006	1,884	Subsea	
1999	Gemini	ChevronTexaco	MC 292	3,393	Subsea	
1999	Genesis	ChevronTexaco	GC 205	2,590	Spar	
1999	Macaroni	Shell	GB 602	3,600	Subsea	
1999	Marlin	BP	VK 915	3,236	TLP	
1999	Penn State	Amerada Hess	GB 216	1,450	Subsea	
1999	Pluto	Mariner	MC 674	2,828	Subsea	Yes
1999	Ursa	Shell	MC 809	3,800	TLP	
1999	Virgo	TotalFinaElf	VK 823	1,130	Fixed Platform	Yes
2000	Allegheny South	Eni	GC 298	3,307	Subsea	
2000	Black Widow	Mariner	EW 966	1,850	Subsea	Yes
2000	Conger	Amerada Hess	GB 215	1,500	Subsea	
2000	Diana	ExxonMobil	EB 945	4,500	Subsea	
2000	Europa	Shell	MC 935	3,870	Subsea	
2000	Hoover	ExxonMobil	AC 25	4,825	Spar	
2000	King	Shell	MC 764	3,250	Subsea	
2000	Northwestern	Amerada Hess	GB 200	1,736	Subsea	Yes
2000	Petronius	ChevronTexaco	VK 786	1,753	Compliant Tower	
2001	Brutus	Shell	GC 158	3,300	TLP	
2001	Crosby	Shell	MC 899	4,400	Subsea	
2001	Einset	Shell	VK 872	3,500	Subsea	Yes
2001	EW 878	Walter	EW 878	1,585	Subsea	Yes
2001	Ladybug	ATP	GB 409	1,355	Subsea	Yes
2001	Marshall	ExxonMobil	EB 949	4,376	Subsea	
2001[1]	MC 68	Walter	MC 68	1,360	Subsea	
2001	Mica	ExxonMobil	MC 211	4,580	Subsea	
2001	Nile	BP	VK 914	3,535	Subsea	
2001	Oregano	Shell	GB 559	3,400	Subsea	
2001	Pilsner	Unocal	EB 205	1,108	Subsea	Yes
2001	Prince	El Paso	EW 1003	1,500	TLP	Yes
2001	Serrano	Shell	GB 516	3,153	Subsea	
2001[2]	Typhoon[10]	ChevronTexaco	GC 237	2,107	TLP	Yes
2002	Aconcagua	TotalFinaElf	MC 305	7,100	Subsea	Yes
2002	Aspen	BP	GC 243	3,065	Subsea	Yes
2002	North Boomvang[7]	Kerr-McGee	EB 643	3,650	Spar	Yes

Year of First Production	Project Name[3]	Operator	Block	Water Depth (ft)[4]	System Type	DWRR[5]
2002	West Boomvang[7]	Kerr-McGee	EB 642	3,678	Subsea	Yes
2002	East Boomvang[7]	Kerr-McGee	EB 688	3,795	Subsea	Yes
2002	Camden Hills	Marathon	MC 348	7,216	Subsea	Yes
2002	Horn Mountain	BP	MC 127	5,400	Spar	Yes
2002	King	BP	MC 84	5,418	Subsea	
2002	King Kong	Mariner	GC 472	3,980	Subsea	Yes
2002	King's Peak	BP	DC 133	6,845	Subsea	Yes
2002	Lost Ark	Noble	EB 421	2,960	Subsea	Yes
2002	Madison	ExxonMobil	AC 24	4,856	Subsea	
2002	Manatee	Shell	GC 155	1,939	Subsea	Yes
2002	Nansen	Kerr-McGee	EB 602	3,685	Spar/subsea	Yes
2002	Navajo	Kerr-McGee	EB 690	4,210	Subsea	Yes
2002	Princess	Shell	MC 765	3,642	Subsea	
2002[1]	Sangria	Hydro GOM	GC 177	1,487	Subsea	Yes
2002	Tulane	Amerada Hess	GB 158	1,054	Subsea	Yes
2002	Yosemite	Mariner	GC 516	4,150	Subsea	Yes
2003[2]	Boris[10]	BHP Billiton	GC 282	2,378	Subsea	Yes
2003	Dawson[8]	Kerr-McGee	GB 669	3,152	Subsea	Yes
2003	Durango[8]	Kerr-McGee	GB 667	3,105	Subsea	Yes
2003	East Anstey/Na Kika	BP	MC 607	6,590	Semisubmersible/ Subsea[6]	
2003	Falcon	Marubeni	EB 579	3,638	Subsea	Yes
2003	Fourier/Na Kika	BP	MC 522	6,940	Semisubmersible/ Subsea[6]	
2003	Gunnison	Kerr-McGee	GB 668	3,058	Spar/subsea	Yes
2003	Habanero	Shell	GB 341	2,015	Subsea	
2003	Herschel/Na Kika	BP	MC 520	6,739	Semisubmersible/ Subsea[6]	
2003	Matterhorn	TotalFinaElf	MC 243	2,850	TLP	Yes
2003	Medusa	Murphy	MC 582	2,223	Spar	Yes
2003	North Medusa	Murphy	MC 538	2,095	Subsea	Yes
2003[2]	Pardner	Anadarko	MC 401	1,139	Subsea	Yes
2003	Tomahawk	Marubeni	EB 623	3,412	Subsea	Yes
2003	Zia	Devon	MC 496	1,804	Subsea	
2004	Ariel/Na Kika	BP	MC 429	6,240	Semisubmersible/ Subsea[6]	
2004	Coulomb/Na Kika	Shell	MC 657	7,591	Semisubmersible/ Subsea[6]	Yes

Year of First Production	Project Name[3]	Operator	Block	Water Depth (ft)[4]	System Type	DWRR[5]
2004	Devil's Tower	Eni	MC 773	5,610	Spar	Yes
2004	Front Runner	Murphy	GC 338	3,330	Spar	Yes
2004	Glider	Shell	GC 248	3,440	Subsea	
2004	Hack Wilson	Kerr-McGee	EB 599	3,650	Subsea	Yes
2004[2]	Harrier	Pioneer	EB 759	4,114	Subsea	Yes
2004	Holstein	BP	GC 645	4,340	Spar	
2004	Kepler/Na Kika	BP	MC 383	5,759	Semisubmersible/ Subsea[6]	
2004	Llano	Shell	GB 386	2,340	Subsea	Yes
2004	Magnolia	ConocoPhillips	GB 783	4,670	TLP	
2004	Marco Polo	Anadarko	GC 608	4,300	TLP	Yes
2004	MC 837	Walter	MC 837	1,524	Subsea	
2004	Ochre	Mariner	MC 66	1,144	Subsea	
2004[2]	Raptor	Pioneer	EB 668	3,710	Subsea	Yes
2004	Red Hawk	Kerr-McGee	GB 876	5,300	Spar	Yes
2004	South Diana	ExxonMobil	AC 65	4,852	Subsea	
2005	Baccarat	W and T Offshore	GC 178	1,404	Subsea	Yes
2005	Citrine	LLOG	GC 157	2,614	Subsea	Yes
2005	GC 137	Nexen	GC 137	1,168	Subsea	Yes
2005	K2	Anadarko	GC 562	4,006	Subsea	
2005	Mad Dog	BP	GC 782	4,420	Spar	
2005	Swordfish	Noble	VK 962	4,677	Subsea	
2005	Triton/Goldfinger	Eni	MC 728	5,610	Subsea	Yes
2006	Constitution	Kerr-McGee	GC 680	4,970	Spar	Yes
2006	Dawson Deep	Kerr-McGee	GB 625	2,965	Subsea	
2006	Gomez	ATP	MC 711	2,975	Semisubmersible	
2006	K2 North	Anadarko	GC 518	4,049	Subsea	Yes
2006	Lorien	Noble	GC 199	2,315	Subsea	
2006	Rigel	Eni	MC 252	5,225	Subsea	Yes
2006	Seventeen Hands	Eni	MC299	5,881	Subsea	Yes
2006	SW Horseshoe	Walter	EB 430	2,285	Subsea	Yes
2006	Ticonderoga	Kerr-McGee	GC 768	5,272	Subsea	Yes
2007	Atlantis	BP	GC 787	7,050	Semisubmersible	
2007	Atlas-Atlas NW/ Ind. Hub	Anadarko	LL 50	8,934	FPS/Subsea[9]	
2007	Cheyenne/Ind. Hub	Anadarko	LL 399	8,951	FPS/Subsea[9]	

Year of First Production	Project Name[3]	Operator	Block	Water Depth (ft)[4]	System Type	DWRR[5]
2007	Cottonwood	Petrobras	GB 244	2,130	Subsea	
2007	Deimos	Shell	MC 806	3,106	Subsea	
2007	Jubilee/Ind. Hub	Anadarko	AT 349	8,825	FPS/Subsea[9]	
2007	Merganser/Ind. Hub	Anadarko	AT 37	8,015	FPS/Subsea[9]	
2007	Mondo NW/Ind. Hub	Anadarko	LL 1	8,340	FPS/Subsea[9]	
2007	Neptune	BHP Billiton	GC 613	4,232	TLP	
2007	Q/Ind. Hub	Statoil Hydro	MC 961	7,925	FPS/Subsea[9]	
2007	San Jacinto/Ind. Hub	Eni	DC 618	7,850	FPS/Subsea[9]	
2007	Shenzi[11]	BHP Billiton	GC 652	4,300	TLP/Subsea	
2007	Spiderman/Ind. Hub	Anadarko	DC 621	8,087	FPS/Subsea[9]	
2007	Vortex/Ind. Hub	Anadarko	AT 261	8,344	FPS/Subsea[9]	
2007	Wrigley	Newfield	MC 506	3,911	Subsea	
2008	Blind Faith	ChevronTexaco	MC 650	6,989	Semisubmersible	
2008	Danny	Remington Oil & Gas	GB 506	2,700	Subsea	
2008[1]	GB 302	Walter	GB 302	2,410	Subsea	
2008	MC 241	Walter	MC 241	2,415		
2008	MC 161	Walter	MC 161	2,924	Subsea	
2008	Mirage	ATP	MC 941	4,000	Spar	
2008[2]	Phoenix[10]	Helix	GC 237	2,679	FPU	
2008	Raton	Nobel	MC 248	3,290		
2008	Thunder Horse	BP	MC 778	6,037	Semisubmersible	
2008	Valley Forge	LLOG	MC 707	1,538	Subsea	
2009	Great White	Shell	AC 857	8,000	Spar	
2009	Isabela	BP	MC 562	6,500	Semisubmersible	
2009	Longhorn	Eni	MC 502	2,442	Subsea	
2009[1]	Morgus	ATP	MC 942	3,960	Subsea	
2009[1]	Navarro	ATP	GC 37	2,019		
2009	Tahiti	ChevronTexaco	GC 641	4,000	Spar	
2009	Telemark	ATP	AT 63	4,385	Subsea	
2009	Thunder Hawk	Murphy	MC 736	6,050	Semisubmersible	
2009	Unreleasable					
2009	Unreleasable					
2010	Cascade	Petrobras	WR 206	8,152	FPS0/Subsea[12]	
2010	Chinook	Petrobras	WR 469	8,831	FPS0/Subsea[12]	
2010	Gotcha Deep	Total	AC 856	7,815		

Year of First Production	Project Name[3]	Operator	Block	Water Depth (ft)[4]	System Type	DWRR[5]
2010	Silvertip	Shell	AC 815	9,226	Subsea	
2010	Tobago	Shell	AC 859	9,627	Subsea	
2010	Unreleasable					
2010	Unreleasable					
2011	Unreleasable					
2011	Unreleasable					
2011	Unreleasable					
2012	Unreleasable					
2013	Puma	BP	GC 823	4,129		
2014	Unreleasable					
2015	Unreleasable					

AC = Alaminos Canyon	AT = Atwater Valley	DC = DeSoto Canyon
EB = East Breaks	EW = Ewing Bank	GB = Garden Banks
GC = Green Canyon	LL = Lloyd Ridge	MC = Mississippi Canyon
VK = Viosca Knoll	WR = Walker Ridge	

[1] Projects off production, lease(s) expired.

[2] Projects off production, lease(s) active.

[3] Editions of this report prior to 2004 listed deepwater fields rather than projects. A block may be listed under more than one project name because of lease relinquishment, expiration, or termination and subsequent re-leasing. Some announced discoveries never reached the project stage and are listed under their prospect names.

[4] Water depths are approximate and may vary depending on the location of the production facility or the location of a well (average of wells or deepest well site).

[5] Indicates projects with one or more leases, which may be subject to thresholds, to receive Deep Water Royalty Relief (DWRR).

[6] Na Kika semisubmersible is located in Mississippi Canyon Block 474 in 6,378 ft (1,944 m) of water.

[7] 2004 Report referred to the entire area as Boomvang.

[8] Included in 2004 Report with Gunnison.

[9] Independence Hub FPS is located in Mississippi Canyon Block 920 in 7,920 ft (2,414 m) of water.

[10] The TLP associated with the Typhoon and Boris projects was destroyed by Hurricane Rita in 2005. Helix is scheduled to redevelop the projects with an FPU by late 2008. The new project name is Phoenix.

[11] The Shenzi project includes the Genghis Khan development. Production commenced from Genghis Khan in October 2007 and will be transported to the Marco Polo TLP in Green Canyon Block 608 in 4,300 ft (1,311 m) of water. The Shenzi portion of the project will feature a TLP in Green Canyon Block 653 in 4,812 ft (1,467 m) of water and is scheduled to commence production in mid-2009.

[12] The Cascade and Chinook Fields will be developed by an FPSO operated by Petrobras. The FPSO will be located in Walker Ridge Block 249 in approximately 8,200 ft (2,499 m) of water.

Appendix B. Lease Sale Related Information

Table B-1. Chronological Listing of GOM Lease Sales by Sale Location and Sale Date

Sale Number	Sale Location	Sale Date	Sale Number	Sale Location	Sale Date
1	LA[1]	10/13/1954	51	TX, LA	12/19/1978
1S	LA	10/13/1954	58	GOM	7/31/1979
2	TX	11/09/1954	58A	GOM	11/27/1979
3	TX, LA	7/12/1955	A62	GOM	9/30/1980
6	LA[2]	8/11/1959	62	GOM	11/18/1980
7	TX, LA	2/24/1960	A66	GOM	7/21/1981
8	LA[3]	5/19/1960	66	GOM	10/20/1981
9	LA	3/13/1962	67	GOM	2/09/1982
10	TX, LA	3/16/1962	69	GOM	11/17/1982
11	LA[2]	10/09/1962	69A	GOM	3/08/1983
12	LA[2]	4/28/1964	72	CGOM	5/25/1983
13	SUL-TX[4]	12/14/1965	74	WGOM	8/24/1983
14	LA[2]	3/29/1966	79	EGOM	1/05/1984
15	LA[2]	10/18/1966	81	CGOM	4/24/1984
16	LA	6/13/1967	84	WGOM	7/18/1984
17	SA-LA[5]	9/05/1967	98	CGOM	5/22/1985
18	TX	5/21/1968	102	WGOM	8/14/1985
19	LA[2]	11/19/1968	94	EGOM	12/18/1985
19A	LA[2]	1/14/1969	104	CGOM	4/30/1986
20	SUL-LA[6]	5/13/1969	105	WGOM	8/27/1986
19B	LA[2]	12/16/1969	110	CGOM	4/22/1987
21	LA[2]	7/21/1970	112	WGOM	8/12/1987
22	LA	12/15/1970	SS[8]	CGOM	2/24/1988
23	LA[2]	11/04/1971	113	CGOM	3/30/1988
24	LA	9/12/1972	115	WGOM	8/31/1988
25	LA	12/19/1972	116	EGOM	11/16/1988
26	TX, LA	6/19/1973	118	CGOM	3/15/1989
32	MAFLA[7]	12/20/1973	122	WGOM	8/23/1989
33	LA	3/28/1974	123	CGOM	3/21/1990
34	TX	5/29/1974	125	WGOM	8/22/1990
S1	TX, LA	7/30/1974	131	CGOM	3/27/1991
36	LA	10/16/1974	135	WGOM	8/21/1991
37	TX	2/04/1975	139	CGOM	5/13/1992
38	TX, LA	5/28/1975	141	WGOM	8/19/1992
38A	TX, LA	7/29/1975	142	CGOM	3/24/1993
41	GOM	2/18/1976	143	WGOM	9/15/1993
44	TX, LA	11/16/1976	147	CGOM	3/30/1994
47	GOM	6/23/1977	150	WGOM	8/17/1994
45	TX, LA	4/25/1978	152	CGOM	5/10/1995
65	GOM	10/31/1978	155	WGOM	9/15/1995

Sale Number	Sale Location	Sale Date
157	CGOM	4/24/1996
161	WGOM	9/25/1996
166	CGOM	3/05/1997
168	WGOM	8/27/1997
169	CGOM	3/18/1998
171	WGOM	8/26/1998
172	CGOM	3/17/1999
174	WGOM	8/25/1999
175	CGOM	3/15/2000
177	WGOM	8/23/2000
178-1	CGOM	3/28/2001
178-2	CGOM	8/22/2001
180	WGOM	8/22/2001

Sale Number	Sale Location	Sale Date
181	EGOM	12/05/2001
182	CGOM	3/20/2002
184	WGOM	8/21/2002
185	CGOM	3/19/2003
187	WGOM	8/20/2003
189	EGOM	12/10/2003
190	CGOM	3/17/2004
192	WGOM	8/18/2004
194	CGOM	3/16/2005
196	WGOM	8/17/2005
197	EGOM	3/16/2005
198	CGOM	3/15/2006
200	WGOM	8/16/2006

[1] Sale 1 was an oil, gas, and sulfur lease sale offshore Louisiana.
[2] These were oil and gas drainage lease sales offshore Louisiana.
[3] Sale 8 was a salt lease sale offshore Louisiana.
[4] Sale 13 was a sulfur and salt lease sale offshore Texas.
[5] Sale 17 was a salt lease sale offshore Louisiana.
[6] Sale 20 was a sulfur and salt lease sale offshore Louisiana.
[7] Sale 32 was an oil and gas lease sale offshore Mississippi, Alabama, and Florida.
[8] Sale SS was a sulfur and salt lease sale in the CGOM.
LA = oil and gas lease sale offshore Louisiana (unless otherwise footnoted)
TX = oil and gas lease sale offshore Texas
GOM = oil and gas lease sale in the Gulf of Mexico
CGOM = oil and gas lease sale in the Central Gulf of Mexico Planning Area
EGOM = oil and gas lease sale in the Eastern Gulf of Mexico Planning Area
WGOM = oil and gas lease sale in the Western Gulf of Mexico Planning Area

Table B-2. Lease Sale Schedule from the 5-Year Program for 2007-2012

Sale Number	Sale Location	Sale Date
204	WGOM	8/22/2007
205	CGOM	10/03/2007
206	CGOM	3/19/2008
224[1]	EGOM	3/19/2008
207	WGOM	2008
208	CGOM	2009
210	WGOM	2009

Sale Number	Sale Location	Sale Date
213	CGOM	2010
215	WGOM	2010
216	CGOM	2011
218	WGOM	2011
220[2]	Mid-Atlantic	2011
222	CGOM	2012

[1] Sale 224 is not a Section 18 sale, but was mandated by Gulf of Mexico Energy Security Act of 2006.
[2] This lease sale would only be held if the President chooses to modify the withdrawal in the area and Congress discontinues the annual appropriations moratorium in the Mid-Atlantic.

APPENDIX C. SUBSEA COMPLETIONS

Area	Block	API Number	Operator	First Completion Date	Water Depth (ft)
AC	24	608054000501	Exxon Mobil Corporation	2/3/2002	4,856
AC	65	608054000302	Exxon Mobil Corporation	12/31/2003	4,852
AT	37	608184003405	Kerr-McGee Oil & Gas Corporation	5/26/2006	7,933
AT	349	608184004500	Anadarko Petroleum Corporation	11/24/2006	8,730
AT	426	608184001701	Mariner Energy Inc	4/3/2007	6,617
AT	574	608184006300	BHP Billiton Petroleum (GOM) Inc	7/4/2007	6,213
AT	574	608184006500	BHP Billiton Petroleum (GOM) Inc	8/15/2007	6,211
AT	575	608184006100	BHP Billiton Petroleum (GOM) Inc	10/10/2007	6,251
BA	A 17	427044034500	Hydro Gulf of Mexico, LLC	8/10/2003	140
DC	133	608234000200	ATP Oil & Gas Corporation	10/15/2001	6,376
DC	618	608234001000	Eni US Operating Co Inc	7/14/2007	7,823
DC	618	608234001200	Eni US Operating Co Inc	6/6/2007	7,787
DC	620	608234000900	Anadarko Petroleum Corporation	8/5/2006	8,055
DC	621	608234000801	Anadarko Petroleum Corporation	9/21/2006	8,087
DC	621	608234001303	Anadarko Petroleum Corporation	3/27/2007	8,087
EB	112	608044015700	Eni US Operating Co Inc	5/1/1996	638
EB	117	608044016102	Apache Corporation	4/11/1996	570
EB	157	608044015200	Eni US Operating Co Inc	5/23/1996	941
EB	161	608044022600	Union Oil Company of California	7/23/2001	1,107
EB	168	608044023000	Walter Oil & Gas Corporation	12/15/2001	500
EB	205	608044021800	Union Oil Company of California	6/1/2001	1,081
EB	430	608044019202	Walter Oil & Gas Corporation	3/13/2005	2,285
EB	464	608044020901	Noble Energy Inc	10/22/2007	2,722
EB	579	608044023500	Marubeni Offshore Production (USA) Inc	11/18/2002	3,453
EB	598	608044025400	Kerr-McGee Oil & Gas Corporation	6/10/2007	3,345
EB	602	608044019001	Kerr-McGee Oil & Gas Corporation	7/15/2001	3,678
EB	602	608044022000	Kerr-McGee Oil & Gas Corporation	8/11/2001	3,678
EB	623	608044023400	Marubeni Offshore Production (USA) Inc	12/30/2002	3,412
EB	646	608044023200	Kerr-McGee Oil & Gas Corporation	4/11/2003	3,905
EB	668	608044024101	Marubeni Offshore Production (USA) Inc	5/26/2005	3,710
EB	688	608044022101	Kerr-McGee Oil & Gas Corporation	1/10/2002	3,788
EB	688	608044022400	Kerr-McGee Oil & Gas Corporation	12/13/2001	3,795
EB	690	608044022801	Kerr-McGee Oil & Gas Corporation	2/18/2002	4,202
EB	759	608044022301	Marubeni Offshore Production (USA) Inc	11/1/2004	4,114
EB	945	608044016200	Exxon Mobil Corporation	3/31/2002	4,628
EB	945	608044017700	Exxon Mobil Corporation	11/20/1999	4,638
EB	945	608044017804	Exxon Mobil Corporation	9/25/2003	4,639
EB	946	608044018000	Exxon Mobil Corporation	5/31/2000	4,657
EB	946	608044018100	Exxon Mobil Corporation	3/8/2000	4,651
EB	948	608044017601	Exxon Mobil Corporation	5/6/2001	4,376
EB	949	608044019301	Exxon Mobil Corporation	4/2/2001	4,376
EC	57	177034047100	Merit Energy Company	12/9/1984	52

Area	Block	API Number	Operator	First Completion Date	Water Depth (ft)
EC	316	177044107400	Remington Oil and Gas Corporation	4/7/2007	201
EC	316	177044109601	Remington Oil and Gas Corporation	10/5/2007	201
EC	335	177044030300	Energy XXI GOM LLC	7/15/1976	272
EC	347	177044101300	Apache Corporation	1/3/2001	291
EC	374	177044101700	Energy Resource Technology Inc	7/17/2002	425
EC	378	608074015700	El Paso E&P Company LP	1/27/1997	495
EI	106	177094121001	Devon Energy Production Company LP	7/20/1998	40
EI	294	177104126801	B T Operating Co	10/6/1991	214
EI	346	177104160500	Apache Corporation	5/10/2006	307
EI	349	177104100500	NCX Company LLC	11/23/1990	337
EI	386	177104147500	Tarpon Offshore LP	2/24/2002	417
EI	390	177104149001	Walter Oil & Gas Corporation	2/11/2004	377
EI	391	177104160200	Remington Oil and Gas Corporation	6/22/2006	398
EI	395	177104157700	Walter Oil & Gas Corporation	3/3/2004	517
EW	868	608104011502	Walter Oil & Gas Corporation	9/21/2004	685
EW	871	608104011000	Walter Oil & Gas Corporation	11/13/2000	932
EW	871	608104011300	Walter Oil & Gas Corporation	4/13/2001	724
EW	878	608105009500	Walter Oil & Gas Corporation	7/26/2000	1,523
EW	878	608105009601	Walter Oil & Gas Corporation	9/25/2000	1,523
EW	878	608105010001	Walter Oil & Gas Corporation	5/13/2007	1,559
EW	913	608104011700	Walter Oil & Gas Corporation	10/13/2004	685
EW	917	608105006500	Marathon Oil Company	4/8/1998	1,195
EW	921	608105007903	Eni US Operating Co Inc	3/29/1999	1,696
EW	921	608105008104	Eni US Operating Co Inc	8/16/2002	1,692
EW	921	608105009801	Eni US Operating Co Inc	1/25/2005	1,712
EW	948	608104012902	Energy XXI GOM LLC	2/10/2007	730
EW	963	608105006000	Marathon Oil Company	5/25/1998	1,740
EW	963	608105006800	Marathon Oil Company	6/29/1998	1,758
EW	966	608104010001	Mariner Energy Inc	5/12/2000	1,853
EW	989	608104013302	W & T Offshore Inc	2/2/2007	523
EW	991	608104009300	Walter Oil & Gas Corporation	7/6/1996	765
EW	1006	608105004102	Walter Oil & Gas Corporation	3/1/2002	1,884
EW	1006	608104012100	Walter Oil & Gas Corporation	6/23/2003	1,851
EW	1006	608104012200	Walter Oil & Gas Corporation	8/27/2003	1,854
GB	108	608074020600	Kerr-McGee Oil & Gas Corporation	7/17/1999	619
GB	117	608074013500	Flextrend Development Company LLC	7/16/1996	922
GB	117	608074014901	Flextrend Development Company LLC	5/5/1997	924
GB	139	608074064501	W & T Offshore Inc	11/25/2002	550
GB	152	608074020800	Walter Oil & Gas Corporation	7/7/1999	619
GB	158	608074021702	Hess Corporation	1/28/2002	1,050
GB	161	608074015801	McMoran Oil & Gas LLC	9/20/1999	972
GB	161	608074017500	McMoran Oil & Gas LLC	11/17/1999	970
GB	184	608074065100	Offshore Shelf LLC	7/12/2000	698
GB	195	608074082800	Mariner Energy Inc	9/5/2007	690
GB	200	608074021100	Hess Corporation	11/29/2000	1,736

Area	Block	API Number	Operator	First Completion Date	Water Depth (ft)
GB	201	608074023701	Hess Corporation	11/2/2002	1,736
GB	201	608074027002	Hess Corporation	9/5/2005	1,736
GB	205	608074027100	Nexen Petroleum USA Inc	8/5/2005	1,330
GB	215	608074020101	Hess Corporation	2/19/2001	1,457
GB	215	608074017202	Hess Corporation	12/30/2002	1,464
GB	216	608074081901	Hess Corporation	5/22/1999	1,456
GB	216	608074022600	Hess Corporation	6/20/2001	1,481
GB	235	608074010600	W & T Offshore Inc	11/10/1994	785
GB	302	608074082700	Walter Oil & Gas Corporation	1/19/2006	2,410
GB	341	608074025401	Shell Offshore Inc	6/14/2003	2,013
GB	341	608074019107	Shell Offshore Inc	10/15/2007	2,006
GB	385	608074023102	Shell Offshore Inc	4/13/2004	2,610
GB	409	608074016300	ATP Oil & Gas Corporation	5/12/2001	1,355
GB	409	608074063501	ATP Oil & Gas Corporation	9/21/2006	1,360
GB	472	608074020903	Shell Offshore Inc	10/21/2001	3,380
GB	506	608074028202	Remington Oil and Gas Corporation	5/15/2007	2,715
GB	506	608074028601	Remington Oil and Gas Corporation	8/13/2007	2,821
GB	516	608074022402	Shell Offshore Inc	11/21/2001	3,400
GB	559	608074019901	Shell Offshore Inc	8/3/2001	3,400
GB	559	608074022103	Shell Offshore Inc	9/2/2001	3,400
GB	559	608074023901	Shell Offshore Inc	3/18/2003	3,393
GB	602	608074014401	Shell Offshore Inc	12/28/1999	3,708
GB	602	608074019401	Shell Offshore Inc	8/16/1999	3,693
GB	602	608074019301	Shell Offshore Inc	2/27/2001	3,708
GB	625	608074066006	Kerr-McGee Oil & Gas Corporation	4/27/2006	2,965
GB	667	608074065803	Kerr-McGee Oil & Gas Corporation	5/20/2003	3,105
GB	668	608074067500	Kerr-McGee Oil & Gas Corporation	1/3/2006	3,137
GB	877	608074023002	Kerr-McGee Oil & Gas Corporation	8/8/2003	5,334
GB	877	608074024402	Kerr-McGee Oil & Gas Corporation	9/6/2003	5,334
GC	20	608114021300	Shell Gulf of Mexico Inc	12/10/1999	880
GC	50	608114038500	Nexen Petroleum USA Inc	5/5/2004	922
GC	50	608114043400	Nexen Petroleum USA Inc	10/5/2005	690
GC	60	608114020101	Mobil Oil Exploration & Production	6/22/1996	868
GC	112	608114024501	Shell Offshore Inc	10/10/1999	1,968
GC	113	608115012701	Marubeni Oil & Gas (USA) Inc	9/1/1999	2,045
GC	113	608115013100	Marubeni Oil & Gas (USA) Inc	7/17/1999	1,968
GC	116	608115008600	Shell Offshore Inc	1/11/1996	2,046
GC	116	608115012200	Shell Offshore Inc	2/14/1998	2,046
GC	137	608114039202	Nexen Petroleum USA Inc	3/31/2004	1,168
GC	155	608114031100	Shell Offshore Inc	6/23/2002	1,939
GC	157	608114037100	LLOG Exploration Offshore Inc	4/25/2005	2,614
GC	157	608114043801	LLOG Exploration Offshore Inc	11/11/2005	2,614
GC	157	608114043900	LLOG Exploration Offshore Inc	5/8/2006	2,614
GC	195	608114037603	Deep Gulf Energy LP	7/11/2006	1,844
GC	200	608114021800	Shell Offshore Inc	11/10/1997	2,670

Area	Block	API Number	Operator	First Completion Date	Water Depth (ft)
GC	200	608114021600	Shell Offshore Inc	12/7/1997	2,670
GC	200	608114020501	Shell Offshore Inc	6/29/1998	2,670
GC	200	608114021901	Shell Offshore Inc	2/27/1999	2,670
GC	200	608114028900	Shell Offshore Inc	1/25/2001	2,672
GC	237	608114024100	Energy Resource Technology Inc	6/13/2001	2,025
GC	237	608114024704	Energy Resource Technology Inc	6/10/2003	1,982
GC	237	608114025203	Energy Resource Technology Inc	9/6/2005	1,987
GC	243	608114034000	Nexen Petroleum USA Inc	12/28/2002	3,048
GC	243	608114041600	Nexen Petroleum USA Inc	7/4/2004	3,050
GC	243	608114045701	Nexen Petroleum USA Inc	11/25/2006	2,980
GC	243	608114027608	Nexen Petroleum USA Inc	7/19/2007	3,048
GC	244	608114021701	Marathon Oil Company	3/2/1998	2,670
GC	254	608115009001	Eni US Operating Co Inc	8/16/2000	3,234
GC	254	608115008001	Eni US Operating Co Inc	11/4/2001	3,226
GC	282	608114030804	Energy Resource Technology Inc	11/22/2002	2,386
GC	282	608114033701	Energy Resource Technology Inc	8/1/2003	2,370
GC	297	608115009400	Eni US Operating Co Inc	9/11/2001	3,308
GC	298	608114042105	Eni US Operating Co Inc	5/20/2006	3,307
GC	338	608114042400	Walter Oil & Gas Corporation	1/11/2007	3,278
GC	473	608114027302	Eni US Operating Co Inc	3/20/2006	3,926
GC	516	608114030101	Eni US Operating Co Inc	10/2/2001	3,839
GC	518	608114039401	Anadarko Petroleum Corporation	7/18/2006	3,993
GC	562	608114036403	Anadarko Petroleum Corporation	4/22/2005	4,006
GC	562	608114033605	Anadarko Petroleum Corporation	7/3/2006	3,925
GC	596	608114035704	Chevron USA Inc	7/3/2007	4,029
GC	640	608114033003	Chevron USA Inc	4/25/2007	4,017
GC	743	608114041200	BP Exploration & Production Inc	4/28/2006	6,830
GC	743	608114040102	BP Exploration & Production Inc	3/18/2007	6,824
GI	32	177174011700	GOM Shelf LLC	3/9/1980	98
HI	A 308	427114085500	Tarpon Operating & Development LLC	8/16/2004	212
HI	A 309	427114070100	SPN Resources LLC	1/24/1995	213
HI	A 336	427114086100	Tarpon Operating & Development LLC	12/31/2004	235
HI	A 343	427114082501	Tarpon Operating & Development LLC	2/26/2005	257
HI	A 345	427114083000	Seneca Resources Corporation	7/26/2003	238
HI	A 378	427114075700	Offshore Shelf LLC	7/28/1996	360
HI	A 466	427094116100	Remington Oil and Gas Corporation	6/23/2007	175
HI	A 531	427094106900	McMoran Oil & Gas LLC	8/25/1999	194
HI	A 531	427094109100	McMoran Oil & Gas LLC	3/24/2001	194
HI	A 540	427094115700	Walter Oil & Gas Corporation	1/4/2006	220
HI	A 544	427094113200	Energy Resource Technology Inc	9/6/2003	234
HI	A 573	427094053700	Apache Corporation	9/17/1980	350
LL	1	608244000401	Anadarko Petroleum Corporation	2/11/2007	8,340
LL	5	608244000200	Anadarko Petroleum Corporation	1/15/2007	8,807
LL	50	608244000101	Anadarko Petroleum Corporation	12/20/2006	8,953
LL	309	608184005200	Anadarko Petroleum Corporation	11/17/2006	8,774

Area	Block	API Number	Operator	First Completion Date	Water Depth (ft)
LL	399	608244000600	Anadarko Petroleum Corporation	10/13/2006	8,960
MC	28	608164018600	BP Exploration & Production Inc	4/21/1995	1,290
MC	28	608174051900	BP Exploration & Production Inc	6/30/1996	1,853
MC	28	608174052000	BP Exploration & Production Inc	4/24/1998	1,853
MC	28	608174051600	BP Exploration & Production Inc	8/16/1996	1,853
MC	28	608174051704	BP Exploration & Production Inc	6/26/2001	1,853
MC	66	608174100101	Mariner Energy Inc	9/3/2003	1,144
MC	68	608174088600	Walter Oil & Gas Corporation	6/3/2000	1,337
MC	72	608174051800	BP Exploration & Production Inc	2/14/1997	1,853
MC	72	608174051500	BP Exploration & Production Inc	4/27/1996	1,853
MC	84	608174096500	BP Exploration & Production Inc	2/5/2003	5,418
MC	85	608174090100	BP Exploration & Production Inc	6/15/2001	5,173
MC	85	608174090801	BP Exploration & Production Inc	5/13/2001	5,317
MC	148	608174109900	Apache Corporation	9/1/2006	550
MC	161	608174106702	Walter Oil & Gas Corporation	8/23/2005	2,924
MC	167	608174088802	Exxon Mobil Corporation	12/29/2004	4,318
MC	211	608174088900	Exxon Mobil Corporation	11/22/2000	4,317
MC	211	608174099200	Exxon Mobil Corporation	8/28/2002	4,318
MC	217	608174090900	ATP Oil & Gas Corporation	1/7/2002	6,390
MC	217	608174091001	ATP Oil & Gas Corporation	8/22/2001	6,420
MC	241	608174111401	Walter Oil & Gas Corporation	4/28/2007	2,427
MC	248	608174109201	Noble Energy Inc	10/13/2007	3,368
MC	278	608174091504	Walter Oil & Gas Corporation	5/24/2005	560
MC	292	608174050900	Noble Energy Inc	5/25/1999	3,405
MC	292	608174083201	Noble Energy Inc	8/25/1999	3,393
MC	292	608174083301	Noble Energy Inc	9/24/1999	3,393
MC	299	608174091202	Eni US Operating Co Inc	5/13/2005	5,881
MC	305	608174083400	ATP Oil & Gas Corporation	7/12/2002	7,073
MC	305	608174091700	ATP Oil & Gas Corporation	5/1/2002	7,096
MC	305	608174098201	ATP Oil & Gas Corporation	8/15/2002	7,067
MC	305	608174087501	ATP Oil & Gas Corporation	9/11/2002	7,001
MC	321	608174089100	Walter Oil & Gas Corporation	9/15/2000	567
MC	322	608174093800	Walter Oil & Gas Corporation	7/8/2001	680
MC	348	608174086801	ATP Oil & Gas Corporation	5/31/2002	7,202
MC	348	608174084801	ATP Oil & Gas Corporation	2/15/2002	7,209
MC	354	608174044700	Exxon Mobil Corporation	7/5/1993	1,460
MC	355	608174044900	Exxon Mobil Corporation	5/29/1993	1,460
MC	355	608174044800	Exxon Mobil Corporation	9/11/1993	1,458
MC	355	608174084301	Exxon Mobil Corporation	7/2/1999	1,458
MC	357	608174053801	Newfield Exploration Company	2/25/1998	445
MC	383	608174094702	BP Exploration & Production Inc	8/26/2002	5,739
MC	383	608174094601	BP Exploration & Production Inc	8/11/2002	5,735
MC	400	608174096101	Apache Corporation	6/13/2005	1,139
MC	429	608174051300	BP Exploration & Production Inc	10/23/2002	6,240
MC	429	608174095402	BP Exploration & Production Inc	2/2/2003	6,101

Area	Block	API Number	Operator	First Completion Date	Water Depth (ft)
MC	429	608174084404	BP Exploration & Production Inc	2/19/2003	6,134
MC	506	608174106101	Newfield Exploration Company	1/20/2007	3,682
MC	520	608174054601	BP Exploration & Production Inc	7/1/2002	6,738
MC	522	608174096900	BP Exploration & Production Inc	11/26/2002	6,932
MC	522	608174097000	BP Exploration & Production Inc	12/16/2002	6,934
MC	522	608174085802	BP Exploration & Production Inc	12/31/2002	6,940
MC	522	608174110100	BP Exploration & Production Inc	7/26/2007	6,933
MC	538	608174101301	Murphy Exploration & Production Co USA	2/16/2005	1,849
MC	608	608174098400	BP Exploration & Production Inc	7/22/2002	6,623
MC	657	608174087203	Shell Offshore Inc	5/1/2004	7,565
MC	661	608174083900	Pogo Producing Company	11/13/2001	854
MC	674	608174054404	Mariner Energy Inc	12/29/1999	2,710
MC	674	608174105502	Mariner Energy Inc	3/22/2005	2,799
MC	686	608174099600	Shell Offshore Inc	3/12/2003	5,318
MC	686	608174110901	Shell Offshore Inc	4/21/2007	5,377
MC	687	608174054000	Shell Offshore Inc	11/20/1998	5,292
MC	705	608174086001	Pogo Producing Company	12/24/2001	854
MC	707	608174103902	LLOG Exploration Offshore Inc	9/11/2007	1,538
MC	711	608174089600	ATP Oil & Gas Corporation	8/11/2006	2,951
MC	711	608174111901	ATP Oil & Gas Corporation	7/26/2007	2,950
MC	730	608174054200	Shell Offshore Inc	11/4/1997	5,295
MC	755	608174057300	ATP Oil & Gas Corporation	12/11/2005	2,975
MC	755	608174106203	ATP Oil & Gas Corporation	3/23/2007	2,904
MC	762	608174111201	Shell Offshore Inc	7/24/2007	2,902
MC	763	608174047700	Shell Offshore Inc	8/8/1997	2,945
MC	764	608174058701	BP Exploration & Production Inc	4/6/2000	3,283
MC	765	608174100501	Shell Offshore Inc	7/18/2003	3,642
MC	765	608174098802	Shell Offshore Inc	12/29/2003	3,642
MC	766	608174096302	Shell Offshore Inc	9/11/2003	3,637
MC	771	608174102404	Eni US Operating Co Inc	1/20/2005	5,413
MC	772	608174099100	Eni US Operating Co Inc	3/16/2005	5,380
MC	777	608174110400	BP Exploration & Production Inc	4/12/2007	5,610
MC	806	608174049501	Shell Offshore Inc	1/3/2005	2,945
MC	806	608174099002	Shell Offshore Inc	4/2/2007	3,003
MC	807	608174038800	Shell Offshore Inc	3/25/1996	2,956
MC	822	608174098601	BP Exploration & Production Inc	11/10/2004	6,034
MC	837	608174092401	Walter Oil & Gas Corporation	6/22/2001	1,524
MC	898	608174106000	Shell Offshore Inc	10/31/2006	4,036
MC	899	608174091600	Shell Offshore Inc	8/13/2001	4,393
MC	899	608174058002	Shell Offshore Inc	7/24/2001	4,393
MC	899	608174087807	Shell Offshore Inc	10/31/2001	4,389
MC	934	608174083501	Shell Offshore Inc	11/13/1999	3,875
MC	934	608174083700	Shell Offshore Inc	9/1/2001	3,875
MC	934	608174083601	Shell Offshore Inc	3/10/2000	3,875
MC	935	608174106800	Shell Offshore Inc	2/4/2006	3,853

Area	Block	API Number	Operator	First Completion Date	Water Depth (ft)
MC	935	608174107300	Shell Offshore Inc	2/28/2006	3,851
MC	961	608174106601	Hydro Gulf of Mexico, LLC	10/10/2007	7,925
MP	149	177254058901	Walter Oil & Gas Corporation	9/6/1994	220
MP	150	177254069600	Walter Oil & Gas Corporation	12/3/2000	245
MP	185	177244091901	Magnum Hunter Production Inc	9/19/2006	155
MP	187	177244092500	Magnum Hunter Production Inc	11/2/2006	142
MP	200	177244092200	Magnum Hunter Production Inc	5/3/2007	163
MP	211	177244093100	Magnum Hunter Production Inc	5/20/2007	178
MP	232	177244093000	Magnum Hunter Production Inc	2/7/2007	178
MP	241	177244092900	Magnum Hunter Production Inc	6/16/2007	186
MP	260	177244081400	Devon Energy Production Company LP	4/26/1999	315
MP	263	177244089600	Magnum Hunter Production Inc	3/31/2003	280
MP	280	177244091200	Dominion Exploration & Production Inc	2/9/2005	307
MU	806	427024024500	Apache Corporation	11/30/1995	164
PN	996	427134009900	Prime Offshore L L C	11/14/2003	159
PN	A 9	427134050200	Newfield Exploration Company	11/5/2003	201
SM	116	177084094000	Remington Oil and Gas Corporation	1/9/2006	196
SM	195	177084093200	Tarpon Operating & Development LLC	2/25/2005	300
SP	32	177212050500	Devon Louisiana Corporation	6/12/2002	115
SS	321	177124057000	ATP Oil & Gas Corporation	5/29/1997	323
ST	177	177154007800	Chevron USA Inc	11/6/1976	144
ST	219	177164033700	Walter Oil & Gas Corporation	3/9/2006	158
ST	248	177164029700	Union Oil Company of California	6/4/2002	178
ST	260	177164029501	Walter Oil & Gas Corporation	5/9/2002	288
ST	288	177164033500	Mariner Energy Inc	2/2/2006	408
VK	738	608164036601	McMoran Oil & Gas LLC	9/24/2000	809
VK	783	608164013401	Shell Offshore Inc	4/8/1991	1,494
VK	783	608164022400	Shell Offshore Inc	12/20/1996	1,451
VK	783	608164022501	Shell Offshore Inc	1/22/1997	1,451
VK	783	608164022301	Shell Offshore Inc	12/20/1996	1,450
VK	783	608164044900	Shell Offshore Inc	10/8/2007	1,142
VK	784	608164023200	Shell Offshore Inc	6/30/1996	1,750
VK	825	608164033201	Kerr-McGee Oil & Gas Corporation	10/16/1998	1,722
VK	825	608164034400	Kerr-McGee Oil & Gas Corporation	8/29/1999	1,711
VK	862	608164021600	Walter Oil & Gas Corporation	11/15/1995	1,067
VK	862	608164044800	Walter Oil & Gas Corporation	7/12/2007	1,060
VK	862	608164044700	Walter Oil & Gas Corporation	7/10/2007	1,060
VK	869	608164042300	Kerr-McGee Oil & Gas Corporation	1/1/2004	2,033
VK	869	608164043000	Kerr-McGee Oil & Gas Corporation	12/29/2004	2,423
VK	873	608164033601	Shell Offshore Inc	12/29/2001	3,463
VK	914	608164028403	BP Exploration & Production Inc	3/15/2001	3,535
VK	915	608164040200	BP Exploration & Production Inc	4/17/2002	3,460
VK	915	608164038301	BP Exploration & Production Inc	8/30/2004	3,460
VK	917	608164040001	Noble Energy Inc	10/4/2007	4,370
VK	961	608164043100	Noble Energy Inc	8/24/2004	4,677

Area	Block	API Number	Operator	First Completion Date	Water Depth (ft)
VK	962	608164039901	Noble Energy Inc	8/24/2004	4,677
VK	986	608164022800	Walter Oil & Gas Corporation	12/23/1995	893
VK	986	608164040800	Walter Oil & Gas Corporation	5/26/2002	895
VK	1003	608164044600	Newfield Exploration Company	5/6/2007	4,858
VR	116	177054107201	W & T Offshore Inc	4/19/1998	55
VR	332	177064091100	Forest Oil Corporation	10/19/2002	223
WC	593	177024182300	Newfield Exploration Company	10/29/2006	253
WC	638	177024116900	McMoran Oil & Gas LLC	11/6/1998	373
WD	45	177190038402	Nexen Petroleum USA Inc	12/8/1981	50
WD	107	177194056400	Walter Oil & Gas Corporation	1/2/1996	222
WD	107	177194058000	Walter Oil & Gas Corporation	2/18/1995	250
WD	107	177194082500	Walter Oil & Gas Corporation	11/4/2006	192

Appendix D. Average Annual GOM Oil and Gas Production

Year	Shallow-Water Oil (MMbbl)	Deepwater Oil (MMbbl)	Total GOM Oil (MMbbl)	Shallow-Water Gas (Bcf)	Deepwater Gas (Bcf)	Total GOM Gas (Bcf)
1947	0	0	0	0	0	0
1948	0	0	0	0	0	0
1949	0	0	0	0	0	0
1950	0	0	0	0	0	0
1951	0	0	0	2	0	2
1952	1	0	1	19	0	19
1953	1	0	1	25	0	25
1954	2	0	2	60	0	60
1955	4	0	4	87	0	87
1956	7	0	7	91	0	91
1957	12	0	12	93	0	93
1958	20	0	20	144	0	144
1959	30	0	30	224	0	224
1960	41	0	41	281	0	281
1961	56	0	56	335	0	335
1962	77	0	77	451	0	451
1963	96	0	96	561	0	561
1964	111	0	111	645	0	645
1965	136	0	136	743	0	743
1966	175	0	175	992	0	992
1967	210	0	210	1,285	0	1,285
1968	254	0	254	1,600	0	1,600
1969	292	0	292	1,950	0	1,950
1970	329	0	329	2,402	0	2,402
1971	376	0	376	2,729	0	2,729
1972	373	0	373	3,004	0	3,004
1973	366	0	366	3,312	0	3,312
1974	338	0	338	3,418	0	3,418
1975	310	0	310	3,427	0	3,427
1976	301	0	301	3,556	0	3,556
1977	284	0	284	3,767	0	3,767
1978	276	0	276	4,244	0	4,244
1979	263	1	263	4,668	0	4,669
1980	260	5	265	4,762	4	4,766
1981	260	4	263	4,886	3	4,888
1982	273	13	286	4,650	16	4,666
1983	294	26	320	4,034	41	4,075
1984	330	25	355	4,525	39	4,564
1985	329	21	350	4,024	34	4,058
1986	336	19	356	4,006	37	4,043
1987	310	17	328	4,481	44	4,525
1988	288	13	301	4,539	38	4,577

Year	Shallow-Water Oil (MMbbl)	Deepwater Oil (MMbbl)	Total GOM Oil (MMbbl)	Shallow-Water Gas (Bcf)	Deepwater Gas (Bcf)	Total GOM Gas (Bcf)
1989	271	10	281	4,604	32	4,636
1990	262	12	275	4,876	31	4,906
1991	272	23	295	4,637	58	4,695
1992	268	37	305	4,555	87	4,642
1993	272	37	309	4,536	120	4,656
1994	272	42	314	4,664	159	4,824
1995	290	55	345	4,598	181	4,779
1996	297	72	369	4,799	278	5,077
1997	303	108	412	4,764	382	5,146
1998	285	159	444	4,481	560	5,042
1999	270	225	495	4,211	846	5,057
2000	252	271	523	3,959	999	4,958
2001	243	315	558	3,879	1,178	5,057
2002	219	348	567	3,237	1,312	4,549
2003	211	350	561	3,000	1,425	4,425
2004	187	348	535	2,604	1,396	4,001
2005	141	326	467	1,960	1,190	3,150
2006	130	343	473	1,818	1,095	2,913

The Department of the Interior Mission

As the Nation's principal conservation agency, the Department of the Interior has responsibility for most of our nationally owned public lands and natural resources. This includes fostering sound use of our land and water resources; protecting our fish, wildlife, and biological diversity; preserving the environmental and cultural values of our national parks and historical places; and providing for the enjoyment of life through outdoor recreation. The Department assesses our energy and mineral resources and works to ensure that their development is in the best interests of all our people by encouraging stewardship and citizen participation in their care. The Department also has a major responsibility for American Indian reservation communities and for people who live in island territories under U.S. administration.

The Minerals Management Service Mission

As a bureau of the Department of the Interior, the Minerals Management Service's (MMS) primary responsibilities are to manage the mineral resources located on the Nation's Outer Continental Shelf (OCS), collect revenue from the Federal OCS and onshore Federal and Indian lands, and distribute those revenues.

Moreover, in working to meet its responsibilities, the **Offshore Minerals Management Program** administers the OCS competitive leasing program and oversees the safe and environmentally sound exploration and production of our Nation's offshore natural gas, oil and other mineral resources. The MMS **Minerals Revenue Management** meets its responsibilities by ensuring the efficient, timely and accurate collection and disbursement of revenue from mineral leasing and production due to Indian tribes and allottees, States and the U.S. Treasury.

The MMS strives to fulfill its responsibilities through the general guiding principles of: (1) being responsive to the public's concerns and interests by maintaining a dialogue with all potentially affected parties and (2) carrying out its programs with an emphasis on working to enhance the quality of life for all Americans by lending MMS assistance and expertise to economic development and environmental protection.